NATURAL DISASTERS

Natural Disasters

Published by Quantum Scientific Publishing a division of Sentient Enterprises, Inc. Pittsburgh, PA. Copyright © 2017 by Sentient Enterprises, Inc. All rights reserved.

table of CONTENTS

Chapter 1 – Introduction to Geological Disasters

Chapter Objective:

- Introduce the various geological disasters and investigate the science of geological disasters

Introduction

Geologic disasters are disasters that involve movement of the Earth. These movements can cause avalanches, earthquakes, tsunamis, and mudflows or lahars. To understand how and why the Earth's surface moves, we must first understand the composition of the planet.

The Earth's layers

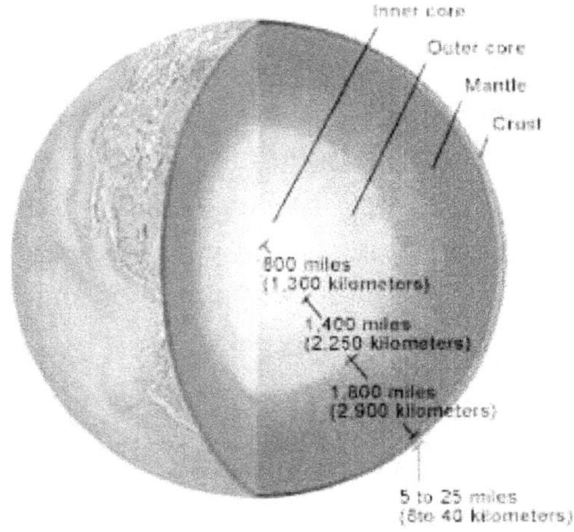

The Earth is a sphere made up of four layers. The innermost layer is the inner core. The inner core is primarily made up of iron and heavy radioactive elements. Although the temperature of the inner core is high enough to melt the iron and other elements, it remains solid because of the great pressure exerted by the other three layers. The outer core is the next layer. The outer core is made up of molten iron, sulfur, and other elements. Although molten, the outer core is slightly cooler than the inner core. Above the outer core is a much thicker, hot layer called the mantle. The temperature of the mantle is over 1,000°C, but it is not hot enough to melt the minerals found in the mantle. The mantle is more like hot plastic, and can be deformed by pressure. The surface layer of the Earth is called the Earth's crust. The crust is solid and brittle, and "floats" on the mantle as a cluster of tectonic plates. Tectonic plates are large sections of the Earth's surface that fit together.

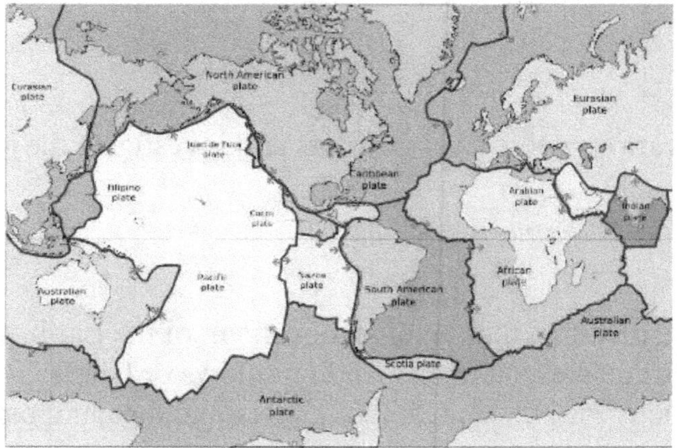

The Earth's surface moves because of the motion of the tectonic plates. Heat rising from the core through the mantle creates regions of increased plasticity. The plates move because the plastic mantle deforms under the pressure of the crust above. The crust is pushed and jostled by lower layers of the crust heating and rising to the surface near the joints between the plates causing them to spread apart. Other plates are pushed beneath each other and recycled to the surface after millions of years. The movements of the Earth's crust are eventually felt on the surface as earthquakes and volcanic eruptions. Earthquakes and volcanic eruptions can drive other events such as avalanches and lahars.

Earthquakes, Tsunamis, Avalanches, and Mudflows or Lahars

Earthquakes are the result of the movement of tectonic plates on the surface of the Earth. As the plates push against each other they stick together briefly and deform. When the tension between the plates grows high enough, they slip past each other or they slip on top of and underneath each other. The slipping is the earthquake. The greater the pressure built up between the plates, the greater the motion of the plates and the more powerful the earthquake.

An avalanche is the movement of snow sliding down the face of a slope. Earthquakes and eruptions can trigger avalanches by shaking the surface layers of soil and rock loose. Heavy rains cause avalanches by increasing the weight of the surface layer and making it more plastic so that it is easier for the surface to start moving. Heavy snowfall on a steep slope can cause an avalanche if too much snow builds up on too steep a surface. Most avalanches are caused by their victims or members of the victim's party.

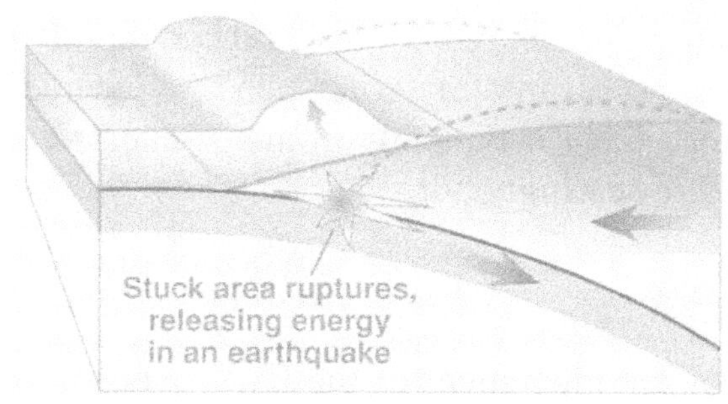

Tsunami

Tsunamis are giant waves caused by earthquakes or volcanic eruptions beneath the ocean. The movement of the Earth beneath the water lifts the water and starts it in motion. As the moving water approaches land, the water near the shore falls back to become part of the growing wall of water. The name *tsunami* is the Japanese word for *harbor wave*. The waves were usually first noticed by fishermen in the harbor because of the seaward movement of the water in the harbor. Tsunamis are also known as tidal waves because the seaward movement of the water near the shore looks like the tide going out quickly. Tsunamis can reach heights of 10 to 100 feet and they flow over the land with tremendous power when they strike.

Lahar from a March 1982 eruption

Mudflows and lahars are movements caused by liquefaction of earth by water. Mudflows are movement of surface materials caused by intense rainfall, sudden overflowing of lakes or bursting of dams. Mudflows are extremely fast and can rapidly bury whatever is in their paths. Lahars are made from volcanic material such as volcanic ash or lava mixed with water. The water source for a lahar is typically from a stream, river, glaciers, or lake water. Lahars move quickly and are searingly hot.

Study of the Earth's movement

Seismology is the study of the movement of the Earth. Seismologists study earthquakes, avalanches, mudflows, and tsunamis. Volcanology is the study of volcanoes, their eruptions, and the materials ejected from a volcano during an eruption, including lahars. Both sciences fall under the more general science of geology. Geologists are scientists who study the Earth in all of its aspects. Many subjects in geology overlap the specific fields of seismology and volcanology. In subsequent chapters we will see how these sciences are used to study geologic disasters in the hopes of reducing the damage they do and saving lives.

Summary

Geologic disasters are disasters caused by movement of the Earth. Earth's movements can cause avalanches, earthquakes, tsunamis, and mudflows or lahars. The Earth is a sphere made up of four layers: the inner core, outer core, mantle, and crust. The Earth's surface moves because of the motion of the tectonic plates. The movements of the Earth's crust are eventually felt on the surface as earthquakes and volcanic eruptions. Seismologists study earthquakes, avalanches, mudflows, and tsunamis. Volcanology is the study of volcanoes. The science that investigates the Earth and its actions is geology.

Concept Reinforcement:

1. What makes the Earth's crust move?

2. What are some of the disasters that can be caused by the movement of the Earth's plates?

3. What is the difference between a seismologist and a volcanologist?

Chapter 2 – Understanding Avalanches

- Explain how scientists measure, monitor and evaluate avalanches

Introduction

Avalanches are usually composed of snow however they can also be made up of soil, rock and other surface materials such as trees. Avalanches occur when the overburdening weight of the material on the surface is too great to remain in place because of the steepness of the slope upon which it rests. Avalanches can be triggered by skiers traveling across steep snowbanks, melting and refreezing of snow layers, heavy rains, and earthquakes. Scientists study avalanches to reduce the likelihood of an avalanche, and to prevent loss of life and property when avalanches do occur.

Measuring avalanches

Snow Avalanche

Avalanches are measured differently in the US, Canada, and Europe.

The measurement of an avalanche in the US is fairly vague and uses a comparative method comparing the size of the avalanche to the size of its path. The size is measured as:

- Sluff, snow that slides less than 150 feet,

- Small, relative to path,

- Medium, relative to path,

- Large relative to path, and

- Major or Maximum relative to path.

The Canadian system describes avalanches by the amount of destruction they may do:

- Relatively harmless to people,

- May bury, injure, or kill a person,

- Could bury or destroy a car, small building, or a few trees,

- Could destroy a railroad car, large truck, several buildings, or cover about 10 acres, and

- Largest known, could destroy a village or cover about 100 acres.

Compare these to the European system that measures the actual physical size of the avalanche as well as the potential damage. The European system has only 4 levels:

- Sluff, cannot bury a person, runs less than 50 m, and has a volume less than 100 cubic meters (m^3),

- Small, stops within the slope, may bury, injure or kill a person, runs less than 100 m, and has a volume less than 1000 m^3,

- Medium, runs to bottom of slope, can bury or destroy a car or break a few trees, runs for less than 1000 m, and has a volume less than 10,000 cubic meters m^3, and

- Large, runs over flat areas and can reach valley floor, can cover buildings, trains, and cover large forested areas, runs for over 1000 m, and has a volume over 10,000 cubic meters m^3.

Monitoring avalanches

The amount of moving material can be measured using Doppler radar imaging. Doppler radar measures the change in the wavelength of radar waves bounced off of a moving object. If the object is moving away, the wavelength of the returning radar signal will be longer. If the object is moving toward the radar receiver, the wavelength of the radar waves will be shorter. Seismographic analysis, in which the sound waves generated by the moving snow are measured as they pass through the Earth causing vibrations, can provide information about the amount of material in the avalanche. Load sensors distributed on a slope can measure the weight of the material passing over them or falling onto them.

Avalanche on Mt. Everest

Authorities monitor avalanches and avalanche conditions to prevent people from entering areas of high avalanche risk and triggering an avalanche. Over 90% of avalanches are triggered by the victims of the avalanche or someone in the victim's group. Noise does not trigger avalanches, contrary to popular belief. Avalanche experts dig snow pits in avalanche country to determine the condition of the snow. Loose layers lying on top of iced over areas are especially prone to sliding. Wind can pile snow into cornices which hang over empty space. If the cornice is too weak to support the weight of a person, it can trigger an avalanche when it is stepped on. Special observers evaluate the size and strength of cornices and other snow structures to determine the avalanche danger.

Evaluating avalanches

Scientists measure the dynamics of avalanches to develop new ways of redirecting avalanches into safer routes or reducing their severity. Avalanche specialists investigate the bottom shear layer of the avalanche, avalanche flow, impact force and effects, erosive effects of avalanches, avalanche dams and their effects, and snow deposition and accumulating forces on avalanches. Scientists measure snow depth, water content, crystal size, slope angle, air temperature and soil temperature, and many other factors to determine the causes of avalanches. They measure the speed of avalanches to determine the forces they may generate. Dry avalanches may reach speeds of 80 mph or more, so don't think about trying to outrun an avalanche!

Summary

Avalanches cause injuries and deaths in snow country every year. Most avalanches are triggered by their victims as they ski, snowmobile, or snowshoe over the snow. Avalanches can block or destroy roads and railways, buildings, and even small towns. Scientists study avalanches to reduce the potential for deadly or economically disastrous slides and to improve safety for winter vacationers. They use Doppler radar, seismographic analysis, load sensors distributed on a slope, snow pits, and visual observation to collect data about snow formations and avalanches. Knowledge of avalanche dynamics has resulted in the placement of avalanche dams and terracing of very steep slopes to prevent or lessen the impact of avalanches in avalanche-prone regions.

Concept Reinforcement:

1. How do the US, Canada, and European avalanche measurement systems differ?

2. What are the tools used by avalanche scientists to monitor avalanches?

3. What are some of the measurements scientists make when evaluating avalanches?

Chapter 3 – Preventing Avalanches

- Understand the role science plays in preventing avalanches

Introduction

Scientists study avalanches to reduce the likelihood of an avalanche, and to prevent loss of life and property when an avalanche occurs. Avalanche science teaches that avalanches are due to slope, load, and weather conditions. While there is little that can be done in regard to weather, slope and load can be altered, and knowledge of weather conditions can be used to close areas of high avalanche danger until authorities have had the opportunity to reduce the danger.

The causes of avalanches

Slope

The steepness, or slope, of the terrain has the greatest impact on whether an avalanche will occur or not. Slopes of less than 25° rarely have avalanches because they are too flat for snow to flow. Slopes above 60° also rarely have avalanches because snow cannot accumulate to any appreciable depth before sliding off. Slopes of 35° to 45° have the greatest likelihood of avalanche caused by people. These slopes are steep enough to ski on, but not so steep as to be avoided by most skiers. Any slope that is steep enough to ski on is steep enough for an avalanche to occur.

The shape of the slope is also important. A concave slope is less likely to contribute to avalanche than a convex slope. Convex slopes make it difficult for lower lying portions of the snowpack to remain connected to higher levels of the snowpack. As the weight of the snow lower on the slope increases it may tear away from the snowpack further up the slope.

Surface cover

Surfaces that are covered with smooth material such as slabs of rock or grass are less able to hold snow in place than surfaces covered with brush, trees, or boulders. The structures beneath the snow serve to hold it more securely and prevent it from sliding.

The condition of the snow overlying the slope is a significant factor in the probability of avalanche. Temperature, precipitation, sun, and wind all affect the snowpack and its stability. Freeze thaw cycles can strengthen the snow by causing it to freeze together, or weaken it by melting it. Long periods of very cold weather can cause the formation of a slippage layer beneath the uppermost layers of the snow. Solar radiation can be absorbed by darker materials under the snow causing melting between layers of snow. Wind can blow and shape snow into cornices and ridges that are brittle and have no underlying support structures. Precipitation in the form of snow can add a layer of snow to the snowpack that is not well bonded to the underlying layers. Sleet, rain, or other precipitation can increase the weight of the snow making it more likely to start sliding, melt the snow, or create a layer of ice that will increase the potential for avalanche of subsequent snowfall.

Avalanche mitigation

Avalanche fence

Because scientists have exposed the causes of avalanches, authorities can take steps to reduce the probability of an avalanche or redirect or reduce its flow. One of the most common techniques used in avalanche country is the use of explosives to start small avalanches. These small avalanches eliminate the build-up of snow so that large avalanches cannot occur. Placement of avalanche fences along steep slopes or potential avalanche paths prevents snow from sliding in much the same way rough terrain prevents snow from sliding. Dams and earthen mounds can be placed in the paths of avalanches to reduce their speed and power or prevent them from reaching important roads, railways, or towns.

Scientists monitor snowpack and avalanche conditions throughout the winter. When the danger of an avalanche begins to increase, authorities are notified and appropriate steps can be taken. Backcountry areas can be closed, explosives can be placed and detonated, and people in danger can be evacuated.

Summary

Scientists study avalanches to reduce the likelihood of an avalanche, and to prevent loss of life and property when avalanches do occur. Avalanche science teaches that avalanches are due to slope, load, and weather conditions. While there is little that can be done in regard to weather, slope can be altered with dams and mounds, and load can be altered with explosions to start small avalanches. Knowledge of weather conditions can be used to close areas of high avalanche danger until authorities have had the opportunity to reduce the danger.

Concept Reinforcement:

1. How does slope affect avalanche danger?

2. What are the conditions of snowpack that contribute to avalanche?

3. How can avalanche danger be minimized?

Chapter 4 – Predicting Avalanches

- Analyze how we can use science to predict avalanches, and prevent catastrophe

Introduction

Scientists use many different strategies to predict avalanches. Scientists use both high tech and low tech methods to examine the snow and calculate avalanche probability. They use pressure plates to measure snowpack load, ground penetrating radar to measure depth and variation of the snowpack, and they dig snow pits to determine the characteristics of the snowpack. Satellite imagery can be used to measure the slope or terrain that is difficult or dangerous to access during the winter. By combining these measures and evaluating the weather, scientists predict when and where avalanches are likely to occur. Steps can then be taken by local authorities to remove the dangers or close the area.

Slope

Scientists use satellite imagery to measure terrain slope and predict avalanche probabilities and paths.

The steepness, or slope, of the terrain has the greatest impact on whether an avalanche will occur or not. Slopes of less than 25° rarely have avalanches because they are too flat for snow to flow. Slopes above 60° also rarely have avalanches because snow cannot accumulate to any appreciable depth before sliding off. Slopes of 35° to 45° have the greatest likelihood of avalanche caused by people. These slopes are steep enough to ski on, but not so steep as to be avoided by most skiers. Any slope that is steep enough to ski on is steep enough for an avalanche to occur.

The shape of the slope is also important. A concave slope is less likely to contribute to avalanche that a convex slope. Convex slopes make it difficult for lower lying portions of the snowpack to remain connected to higher levels of the snowpack. As the weight of the snow lower on the slope increases it may tear away from the snowpack further up the slope.

Scientists map out the slopes' steepness and topography, or shape, and predict the likelihood of an avalanche based on these factors. They create computer models that permit them to input weather and snowpack conditions so they can include these factors in their prediction. When the computer model indicates avalanche danger is high, recommendations to reduce the danger are made and executed.

Snow depth

Use of ground penetrating radar. This is used to measure the depth of snow packs

The depth of the snow is an important factor in determining the load on the slope. The load is important when comparing the tensile strength of the snow, its ability to resist breaking free when pulled, versus its downward pressure. The downward pressure is important in determining the frictional force helping to hold the snow in place. However, increased load also increases the strain on the snowpack to hold together and lowers its tensile strength. Once load has reached the tensile strength limit, the snowpack will crack and an avalanche will occur.

Snowpack conditions

The condition of the snow overlying the slope is a significant factor in the probability of avalanche. Temperature, precipitation, sun, and wind all affect the snowpack and its stability. Freeze thaw cycles can strengthen the snow by causing it to freeze together, or weaken it by melting it. Long periods of very cold weather can cause the formation of a slippage layer beneath the uppermost layers of the snow. Solar radiation can be absorbed by darker materials under the snow causing melting between layers of snow. Wind can blow and shape snow into cornices and ridges that are brittle and have no underlying support structures. Precipitation in the form of snow can add a layer of snow to the snowpack that is not well bonded to the underlying layers. Sleet, rain, or other precipitation can increase the weight of the snow making it more likely to start sliding, melt the snow, or create a layer of ice that will increase the potential for avalanche of subsequent snowfall.

Scientists dig pits in the snowpack to examine the different layers of the pack. They look for ice layers between layers of poorly adherent snow that can serve as an indicator of potential avalanche. They collect samples of snow from various depths of the snowpack to examine the crystalline structure. Large crystals do not hold together as well as small snow crystals, increasing the danger of avalanche. Stress lines and cracks in various layers of the snowpack can show stresses being placed on the snow that might contribute to avalanche danger. The engineers who dig and examine snow pits are highly trained professionals, and rarely become victims of an avalanche. However, amateurs could easily initiate the very avalanche they are investigating if they do not have the detailed knowledge of snow and snowpack conditions to prevent their snow pit from causing enough additional stress to start an avalanche.

Summary

Scientists use many different strategies to predict avalanches. Scientists use pressure plates to measure snowpack load, ground penetrating radar to measure depth and variation of the snowpack, and they dig snow pits to determine the characteristics of the snowpack. Satellite imagery can be used to measure the slope or terrain that is difficult or dangerous to access during the winter. Steep slopes, heavy snow loads, and conditions within the snowpack all contribute to increased risk of avalanche. By combining these measures and evaluating the weather, scientists predict when and where avalanches are likely to occur. Steps can then be taken by local authorities to remove the dangers or close the area.

Concept Reinforcement:

1. How do scientists use topography to evaluate avalanche risk?

2. How does load affect the risk of avalanche?

3. What are some of the characteristics of the snowpack that contribute to avalanche risk?

Chapter 5 – Understanding Earthquakes

Chapter Objective:

- Explain how scientists measure, monitor and evaluate earthquakes

Introduction

Earthquakes take place along tectonic plate boundaries where the Earth's crustal plates slide past or over and under each other. As the plates move, they stick together for relatively brief periods of time. As the tension increases between the moving plates, they slip suddenly, called a fault rupture, resulting in an earthquake. Because earthquakes are so powerful and create so much damage in heavily populated areas, scientists measure, monitor, and evaluate earthquakes to try to predict when the next earthquake will strike. Scientists use seismographs, strain meters, geodetic instruments, and satellite mapping and imagery to measure, monitor, and evaluate earthquakes.

Seismographs

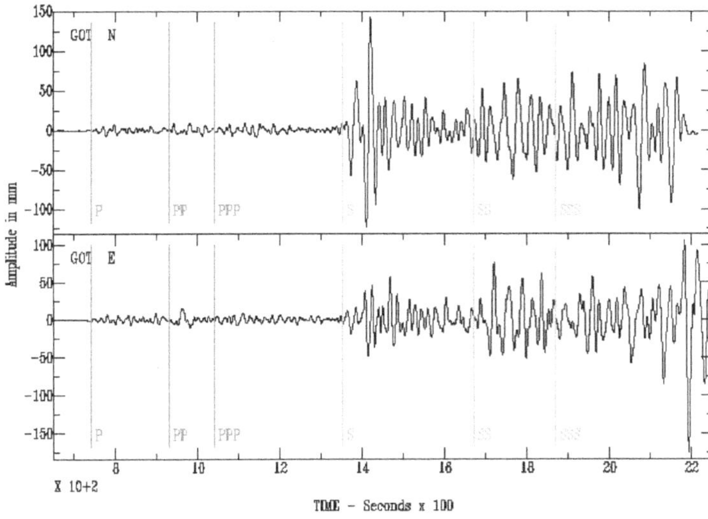

Seismographic output from the 1906 San Francisco earthquake.

Seismographs are sensitive instruments that measure the movement of the Earth's crust during an earthquake. When the Earth slips during an earthquake, the Earth's crust vibrates, or shakes, creating waves that move through the Earth just like sound waves propagate through air. By placing numerous seismographs on the Earth's surface, the strength and direction of the waves generated by the earthquake can be measured. Each wave perturbs a needle bearing a pen that marks on a sheet of graph paper the severity of the perturbance. Most pen and paper seismographs are being replaced with computerized seismographs that can transmit their data over the internet to a central lab. Examining the strength and arrival times of the waves at each seismograph allows seismologists, scientists who study earthquakes, to determine the exact location where the quake originated and its strength.

Strain meters are small laser instruments that are placed in boreholes in areas of seismic activity to measure the changes in tension on the crust of the Earth where they are located. As the tectonic plates move in relation to one another, they deform along their edges as frictional forces hold the plates in place. As the crust is deformed, the light from the laser is displaced across the strain meter. The stress can be measured by measuring the displacement of laser light across detectors in the strain meter. As the stress along a fault increases, the probability of an earthquake increases. Higher stresses before an earthquake indicate the likelihood of a more violent earthquake.

Geodetic measurements

Geodetic measurements are conducted using Global Positioning Satellite (GPS) data, or survey instruments to mark the location of specific points on the surface of the Earth. In areas of seismic activity, these geodetic points move in relation to one another because of the movement of the tectonic plates upon which they rest. Measuring the distance separating the points, which can include height as well as movement in the XY plane, gives seismologists an indication of the speed with which the plates are moving relative to one another. It also tells them how far each plate has moved relative to the other in the event of an earthquake. It is not uncommon to find small bronze plates in National Forests and along fault lines that are emblazoned with the latitude and longitude of the plate when it was placed. The location of the plate can be measured from time to time to determine whether or not it has moved.

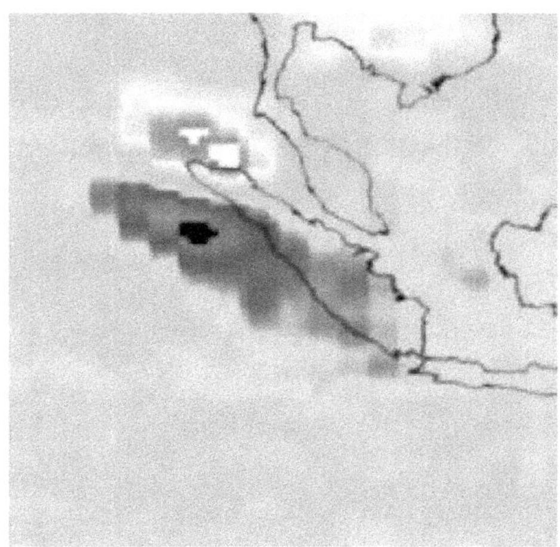

Change in gravitational field in Sumatra due to an earthquake.

Satellite imagery can be used in much the same way as geodetic information. However, satellite imagery can provide images of what is occurring beneath the surface as well. The effects of strain can be seen in changes to landforms farther away from the fault lines. Satellite imagery can also detect changes in gravitational forces, as seen in the figure. Satellite imagery is beneficial in that it can be readily accessed, whereas many geodetic markers require arduous treks to remote locations to determine their movement.

Summary

Earthquakes take place along tectonic plate boundaries where the Earth's crustal plates slide past or over and under each other. As the plates move, they stick together for relatively brief periods of time. As the tension increases between the moving plates, they eventually slip suddenly resulting in an earthquake. Because earthquakes are so powerful and create so much damage in heavily populated areas, scientists measure, monitor, and evaluate earthquakes to try to predict when the next earthquake will strike. Scientists use seismographs, strain meters, geodetic instruments, and satellite mapping and imagery to measure, monitor, and evaluate earthquakes.

Concept Reinforcement:

1. What is a seismograph?

2. How do geodetic measurements help seismologists study earthquakes?

3. How is satellite imagery different from geodetic measurements in the information it provides seismologists?

Chapter 6 – Predicting Earthquakes

Chapter Objective:

- Understand the role science plays in predicting earthquakes

Introduction

A prediction of an earthquake includes when it will occur, where it will occur, why it will occur, the magnitude of the predicted quake, and the probability of the earthquake occurring. At present, seismologists do not make earthquake predictions. The data describing events that might signal an impending earthquake are sketchy. Seismologists may not even know what to measure as a predictor of earthquakes. Changing water levels in wells, unusual behavior of animals, changes in electromagnetic fields in the Earth, tidal activity, and emission of gasses from the Earth have all been postulated as potential harbingers of an earthquake.

However, scientific examination of all of these events and others has eliminated them from consideration as predictors of earthquakes. Instead of predicting earthquakes, seismologists create earthquake forecasts. Earthquakes are forecast to occur within a defined geographic area, with a narrowly defined strength range, over a relatively long timespan in human terms (decades), with a specific level of statistical probability.

Difficulty of earthquake prediction

Earthquake prediction is difficult for many reasons. Because there is currently no way of knowing what signals an approaching earthquake, collecting specific measurements in the earthquake area before the earthquake occurs is not possible. Compounding the problem is that little is known about what signals an approaching earthquake; no one knows what *should* be measured. High magnitude earthquakes are relatively rare phenomena. The rarity of earthquakes, while a blessing to civilization, makes data collection difficult and reduces the statistical validity of the observations. In other words, scientists cannot determine whether what they observed was a true indicator of an earthquake or a phenomenon that occurred by chance.

Potential indicators of an impending earthquake

There are several phenomena that may be indicators of an impending earthquake. However, additional research is necessary to confirm their status as warnings of approaching earthquakes.

Demeter Satellite

Electromagnetic activity in the Earth's crust in the neighborhood of an incipient quake appears to change. Very Low Frequency (VLF) or Ultra Low Frequency (ULF) electromagnetic emissions from the Earth in the neighborhood of an earthquake have been reported for several earthquakes over the past several decades. These VLF and ULF emissions cause changes in the ionosphere, a layer of the atmosphere, which can be detected by satellites in low orbits. The Centre National d'Études Spatiales (CNES) of France launched a small satellite, Detection of Electro-Magnetic Emissions Transmitted from Earthquake Regions (DEMETER), in June of 2004 to study the ionospheric disturbances in an attempt to correlate them with earthquakes. The results have raised more questions than they have answered. Additional studies will have to be completed before electromagnetic disturbances in the ionosphere can be confirmed as a warning of impending quake activity.

Some minerals, most notably quartz, are capable of generating an electrical potential when they are stressed. The resultant voltage is called a piezoelectric charge. Quartz crystals within the Earth's crust may generate piezoelectric charges when they are stressed along a fault before the fault slips and an earthquake ensues. Some scientists have hypothesized that changes in electrical potential in the Earth's crust may signal an approaching earthquake. Metal rods inserted into the Earth and connected to voltmeters can detect changes in electrical currents in the Earth. However, these changes may or may not correspond to impending earthquakes.

Early detection of earthquakes

It is possible to detect some of the fastest moving energy waves generated by an earthquake, so called *primary waves*, which are not destructive, before the destructive *secondary and Rayleigh waves* arrive. The difference in arrival time is only a matter of a few seconds, but that few seconds can be used by automated equipment to shut down high power electrical transmission lines, gas pumping stations, water mains, and other vital infrastructure to reduce the probability of fires, explosions, and electrocutions. QuakeGuard™ is a system that connects to municipal and corporate systems to do just that. QuakeAlarm™ is a home use system that may provide just enough warning for a family to take cover under heavy furniture before the earthquake strikes.

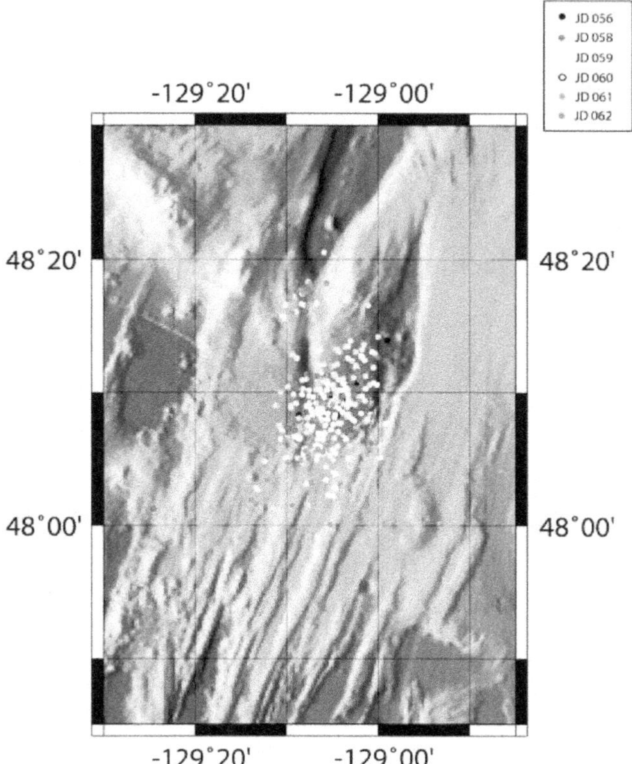

Earthquake swarm along the Juan de Fuca tectonic plate from Feb 25 to Mar 3, 2005. Each dot represents a different epicenter. Diferent colors represent different days.

Earthquakes appear to be generated in clusters or "swarms." Scientists believe that when an earthquake along one portion of a fault line occurs, it transfers some of the stress to other portions of the fault, increasing the potential for an earthquake in a nearby location. While they may be able to predict that additional quakes will occur, they cannot predict when or how large.

Summary

Predicting earthquakes remains the province of psychics and pseudo-science, with little scientific evidence to support any of the claims made by so-called earthquake predictors to date. A prediction of an earthquake includes when it will occur, where it will occur, why it will occur, the magnitude of the predicted quake, and the probability of the earthquake occurring.

At present, seismologists do not make earthquake predictions. The data describing events that might signal an impending earthquake are sketchy. Seismologists may not even know what to measure as a predictor of earthquakes. Instead of predicting earthquakes, seismologists create earthquake forecasts. Earthquakes are forecast to occur within a defined geographic area, with a narrowly defined strength range, over a relatively long timespan in human terms (decades), with a specific level of statistical probability.

Concept Reinforcement:

1. Why is it so difficult to collect the data needed to predict earthquakes?

2. What are the electromagnetic and electrical signals that may indicate an impending earthquake?

3. What is the benefit of detecting an earthquake that is only seconds away?

Chapter 7 – Preventing Earthquake Catastrophes

- Analyze how we can use science to predict earthquakes, and prevent catastrophe

Introduction

Seismology has not advanced to the point yet at which it is capable of predicting earthquakes with any certainty. Instead, seismologists forecast the probability that an earthquake of a certain magnitude will occur in an area over a period of several decades. They may also be able to predict the general direction of the ground shaking of the earth, side to side or up and down. Such forecasts are of little value in issuing evacuation orders or moving emergency response crews into position to respond to an immediate crisis. However, they can be used to avert catastrophe by providing urban planners and civil engineers with the knowledge of the force of an impending quake that buildings and infrastructure must be capable of withstanding. New building codes can be developed, new building projects can be built to higher standards, and older structures can be retrofitted to improve their safety. Early detection of earthquakes is another potentially useful tool in reducing damage.

Building codes and new projects

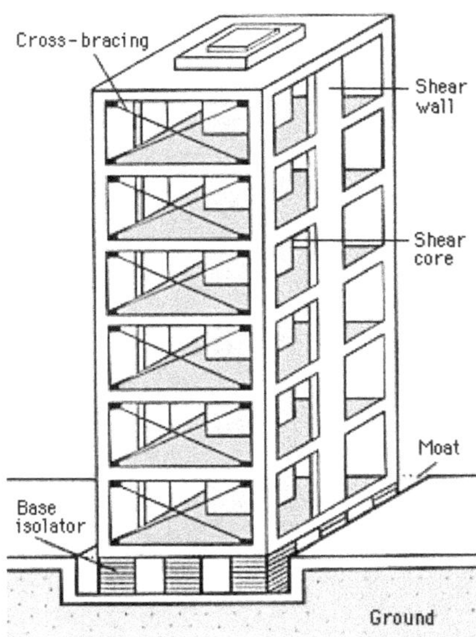

Earthquake-resistant building

Building codes are designed to ensure the survival of a building in the event of "The Big One"; the largest magnitude quake expected in the region. This does not mean there will be no damage to the building, no building can be built that will withstand a massive earthquake completely. But the building will protect its occupants and remain structurally sound despite the damage it sustains. The direction of ground shake is important to consider when proposing new building codes. Lateral shake requires buildings that can withstand sway.

The buildings should be designed to flex slightly, be isolated from the ground, or contain oscillation dampers to counter the lateral movement of the ground. Vertical shake can be compensated by requiring installation of shock absorbers on structures to allow various parts to move slightly in isolation from one another.

Seismic retrofitting

Older structures that were built prior to the knowledge of an impending earthquake or before available technology could compensate for the force of an earthquake can be retrofitted based on earthquake forecasts and the structural stability of the existing structure. There are many techniques to strengthen structures. Reinforcing and bracing support columns, adding interior shear trusses, improved connection between buildings and their additions, removing hot rivets and replacing them with bolts, adding expansion rockers, and reinforced connections can improve the structural stability of existing buildings and bridges. Automatic shut-off valves should be added to gas pipes to prevent the flow of gas from broken pipes and reduce the risk of fire.

Early detection and warning systems

While not earthquake prediction *per se*, it is possible to detect some of the fastest moving energy waves generated by an earthquake, so called *primary waves*, which are not destructive, before the destructive *secondary and Rayleigh waves* arrive. The difference in arrival time is only a matter of a few seconds, but that few seconds can be used by automated equipment to shut down high power electrical transmission lines, gas pumping stations, water mains, and other vital infrastructure to reduce the probability of fires, explosions, and electrocutions. Rapid transit systems can be shut down and trains can be slowed if not stopped in the event of an earthquake. Workers involved in hazardous operations could potentially act to reduce their danger. Surgeons in an operation could remove sharp instruments from patients' bodies. Such a system is currently in use in Japan, Taiwan, Mexico, Turkey, and Romania and is being tested in California.

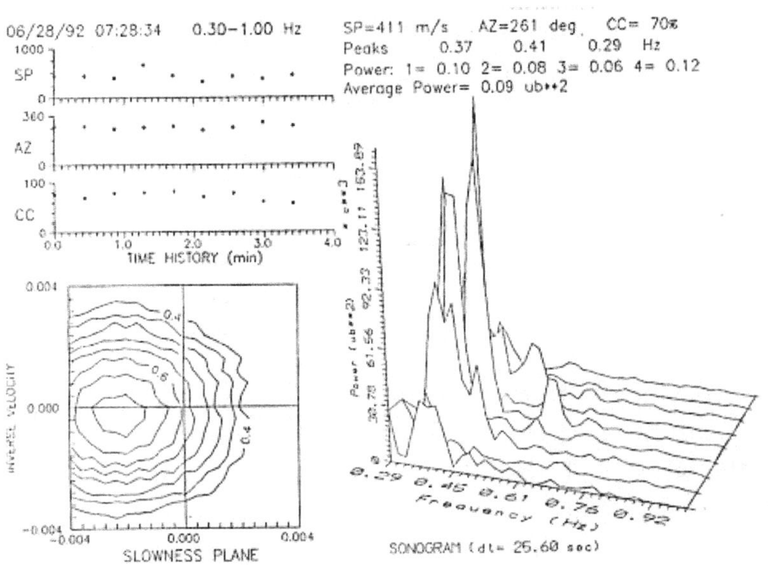

Detected infrasound from earthquake epicenters

Summary

Seismology has not advanced to the point yet at which it is capable of predicting earthquakes with any certainty. Instead, seismologists forecast the probability that an earthquake of a certain magnitude will occur in an area over a period of several decades. Such forecasts can be used to avert catastrophe by providing urban planners and civil engineers with the knowledge of the force of an impending quake that buildings and infrastructure must be capable of withstanding. New building codes can be developed, new building projects can be built to higher standards, and older structures can be retrofitted to improve their safety. Early detection can reduce damage and save lives as well.

Concept Reinforcement:

1. How should new structures be designed to reduce the damage inflicted by an earthquake?

2. How can existing structures be modified to strengthen them against earthquake damage?

3. How does earthquake detection work?

Chapter 8 – Understanding Tsunamis

- Explain how scientists measure, monitor and evaluate tsunamis

Introduction

Tsunami is a Japanese word that translates as "harbor wave." Japanese fishermen were usually the first to notice the drop in water level in the harbor as the ocean rushed out to become part of the incoming wave. They are also referred to as "tidal waves" because the rushing of the ocean away from the shore resembles a fast tide going out. However, the name tidal wave has been discarded in technical usage because it is somewhat misleading. Tsunamis are not generated by the Earth's tides. Instead, they are caused by earthquakes beneath the ocean or massive landslides on the ocean floor.

Tsunami

It is difficult to visually detect a tsunami in the deep ocean. Tsunamis are remarkably simi-lar to surface waves when they are far from land. However, surface waves are generated by wind and their energy does not reach far below the surface. Tsunamis, on the other hand, are generated by movement deep in the ocean and result from the lifting of a column of water that reaches from the bottom of the ocean to the surface. As the wave approaches shallow water near the shore, the column is forced upward into the air. Tsunamis can reach heights of over 100 feet and can rush inland for miles in low-lying coastal areas.

In addition to the massive damage the power of the oncoming wave does as the tsunami crashes over the land, greater damage is done as the ocean recedes and people, animals, and objects are pulled out to sea with it. Because of the destructive power of tsunamis, government and university scientists measure, monitor, and evaluate tsunamis in the hope of mitigating the damage and loss of life they can cause.

Tsunami buoy (maroon in rear) and pressure sensors (4 platforms in foreground) ready for loading on board ship.

Tsunamis are measured by buoys and pressure-sensitive monitors located on the ocean floor known as the Deep ocean Assessment and Reporting of Tsunamis (DART) System. As the wave passes over the monitor, the pressure of the ocean on the monitor increases significantly. When the pressure reaches a threshold value that indicates with high probability that a tsunami has passed over the monitor, the monitor sends a signal to a buoy that is anchored nearby. The buoy then transmits a signal to a satellite relay and the information is relayed to government and university laboratories around the world. Scientists can measure the change in ocean pressure as well as the direction and speed of the tsunami as it passes over neighboring pressure monitors. The pressure differential gives scientists an indication of the magnitude of the oncoming tsunami. By measuring the time it takes for the tsunami to reach nearby pressure monitors and dividing the distance between the monitors by that time, scientists can determine the speed and direction of the tsunami.

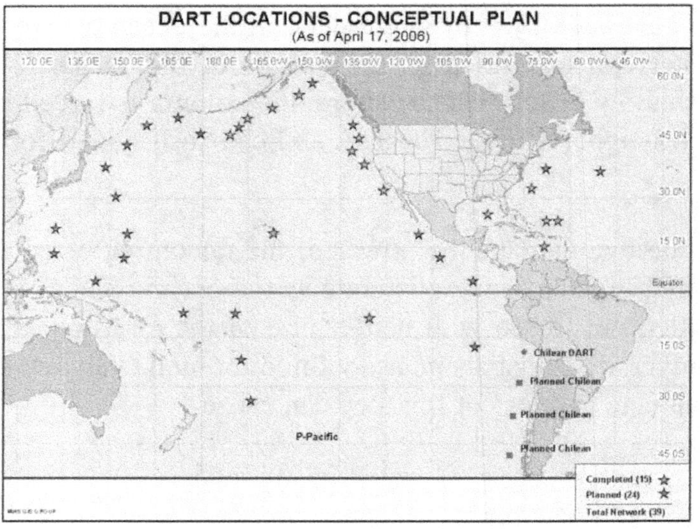

Scientists use a combination of seismic data and information from the DART system to track a tsunami's movement. Tsunamis have been known to travel from the South Polar seas to the North Pole and around the globe. Monitoring stations are either already in place or planned for the entire Pacific basin because of its high level of seismic activity.

Scientists can evaluate the danger posed by tsunamis by combining information from DART with topographical information about the land along the shore. Scientists use the pressure information from DART to estimate the size of the water column. They determine the speed of the oncoming wave using DART information as well. From the size and speed of the oncoming wave, they can estimate the change in sea level to be anticipated where the tsunami strikes land. The topography of the land is then examined to estimate how much land will be covered by the in-rushing ocean. Land that is flat or gently sloped will be inundated for a greater distance inland than land that rises steeply from the ocean. Some harbors can act to channel the tsunami into a small space, concentrating the power of the tsunami with terrible results. The Lituya Bay, tsunami of 1958 in Alaska reached a height of over 1,700 feet, more than a quarter of a mile when it crashed against the steep shore.

Summary

Tsunamis are giant waves generated by earthquakes and massive undersea landslides. Tsunamis are capable of traveling around the world, and crash into the shore with devastating force. Scientists measure tsunamis using pressure sensitive monitors on the ocean floor. As a tsunami passes over a plate, the ocean pressure on the plate changes. The magnitude of the pressure change and the speed with which the pressure wave reaches nearby DART monitors give scientists an indication of the size, direction, and danger of the oncoming tsunami. Scientists can compare this data with topographical information for the shore of the land in the path of the tsunami to estimate the area of land that will be inundated by the wave.

Concept Reinforcement:

1. How is a tsunami generated?

2. How do scientists use the DART system to determine the size of an oncoming tsunami?

3. How do scientists determine the speed and direction of a tsunami?

Chapter 9 – Predicting Tsunamis

Chapter Objective:

- Analyze how we can use science to predict tsunamis, and prevent catastrophe

Introduction

Tsunamis are giant ocean waves caused by earthquakes beneath the ocean or massive landslides on the ocean floor. Tsunamis can rush inland for miles along a shoreline, destroying property and taking lives as it passes over the land and then withdraws, taking much of what it passed over out to sea with it as it recedes. Because of the potential for massive loss of life, governments around the world have joined to create a tsunami detection and forecasting system to provide an early warning to coastal residents.

Predicting tsunamis

Because tsunamis are generated by seismic activity, the first warning of a tsunami generally comes from seismometers that monitor earthquake activity around the world. Seismic waves travel through the Earth many times faster than water forming a tsunami wave can travel. When seismologists detect an earthquake or other seismic event beneath the ocean, they begin trying to determine whether a dangerous tsunami may develop. Many seismic events beneath the ocean are simply too small to create a tsunami that will endanger populations along the coast.

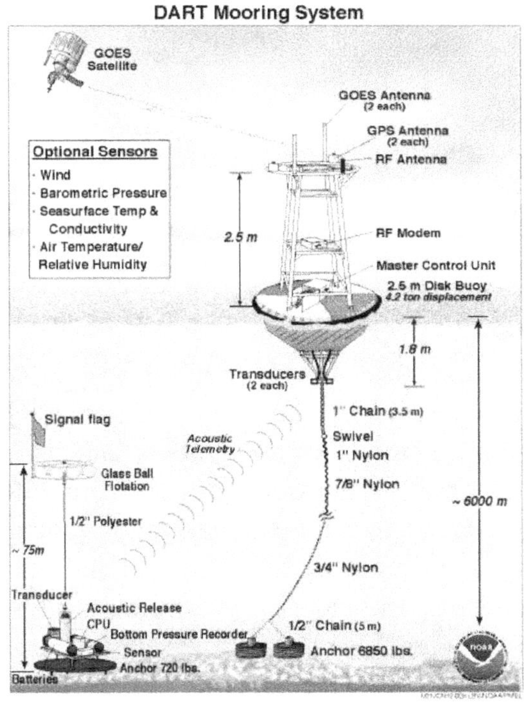

Governments have distributed a system of pressure sensitive monitors, the Deep ocean Assessment and Reporting of Tsunamis (DART) System, to detect tsunamis. As the wave passes over the monitor, the pressure of the ocean on the monitor increases significantly. The monitor sends a signal to a buoy that is anchored nearby which transmits a signal to a satellite relay. The information is relayed to government and university laboratories around the world. With this information, scientists can measure the magnitude, direction, and speed of the oncoming tsunami.

Scientists use a combination of seismic data and information from the DART system to track a tsunami's movement. Scientists have already developed inundation probability maps of coastal areas around the world based on topographical information. Once they know the magnitude and speed of the approaching tsunami and its likely destination, they use the inundation maps to predict the area that will be inundated by the tsunami and the time it can be expected to arrive.

Preventing catastrophe

Coastal areas that are vulnerable to tsunamis are thoroughly mapped, and "safe" areas are indicated on the maps for local authorities. When a tsunami is detected and is predicted to strike a shoreline, warnings are immediately signaled to the local authorities so that residents can be evacuated. Authorities are informed of the predicted inundation area and advised to move people to predetermined safe areas.

Preventing catastrophe is more than simply evacuating people in the path of a tsunami. Tsunamis are periodic events which can be anticipated just as earthquakes are anticipated in earthquake-prone regions of the globe. Scientists can use historic data including archaeological information to predict the frequency and magnitude of tsunamis in a given populated zone. Building codes and land use plans can be developed to ensure that structures built in the path of tsunamis are capable of withstanding their force. Land in the path of tsunamis can be designated parkland or agricultural and timberland to reduce the economic loss in the event of a tsunami. Emergency response supplies and economic recovery plans and resources can be pre-placed near tsunami-prone areas to speed the response to a tsunami. The United States' National Oceanic and Atmospheric Administration (NOAA, pronounced Noah) has created a TsunamiReady Community program to help local officials prepare for a tsunami in their area.

Summary

Tsunamis are giant ocean waves caused by earthquakes beneath the ocean or massive landslides on the ocean floor. Because of the potential for massive loss of life, governments around the world have joined to create a tsunami detection and forecasting system to provide early warning to coastal residents. Seismic information combined with information from pressure sensitive monitors placed along the ocean floor tell scientists the magnitude of an approaching tsunami and where and when it will strike. Emergency preparedness plans for coastlines vulnerable to tsunamis have been developed and can be implemented the moment a tsunami is forecast to strike the area. Scientists use topographical maps and historic and archaeological data to determine the likely area of inundation of approaching tsunamis, and residents are warned to flee to safe areas.

Concept Reinforcement:

1. How can scientists use topographical, historical, and archaeological information to improve safety in the event of a tsunami?

2. How can authorities reduce the loss of life resulting from tsunamis using scientific information?

3. How can authorities reduce property damage resulting from tsunamis using scientific information?

igniting anything in its path. Still others, like Mount St. Helens, erupt so violently that the side of the mountain fails, and the mountain blasts enormous portions of itself into the air before collapsing on one or several sides.

Summary

Volcanoes are the results of weak spots in the Earth's crust that rupture allowing molten rock, or lava, and gasses to escape from the lower lithosphere and upper mantle of the Earth. Volcanologists measure, monitor, and evaluate seismic activity, ground deformation, and gas emissions from a volcano to determine whether an eruption is imminent. Volcanologists also use their measurements to predict the type of eruption that will occur and the potential path of destruction it will produce.

Concept Reinforcement:

1. What are the three areas where volcanoes are found?

2. How do scientists monitor volcanoes?

3. What predictions can scientists make from their measurements?

Chapter 11 – Predicting Volcanic Eruptions

*   Understand the role science plays in predicting volcanic eruptions

Introduction

Volcanoes can lie dormant for hundreds to tens of thousands of years, giving no sign of life, then suddenly awaken to cause massive damage and change the planet's climate. While such a time span may appear to be very long to humans, the Earth is over 4 billion years old. To put 10,000 years in perspective to the age of the Earth, the equivalent time in a human life of 75 years would be 98.55 minutes. An hour and a half is no more than a nap in the life of a human, 10,000 years is a short nap for the Earth. How many times, in the course of a nap might a person twitch without awakening? The same is true of volcanoes, and people become accustomed to the slight tremors and ventings of nearby volcanoes. When the volcano finally awakens, people who have ignored the warnings are caught in the devastation, as were the people of Pompeii when Mt. Vesuvius erupted in 79 C.E. The devastation that can be caused by a volcano and the difficulty in understanding such a long-lived feature compared to human lifetimes requires the application of science to provide warning of impending disaster.

The Eruption of Mount Vesuvius

Predicting volcanic eruptions

Volcanologists monitor the movement of magma beneath the volcano by the earthquake swarms and other seismic events it generates. Seismographic equipment placed on the surface of the volcano and the surrounding area record seismic activity. Increased seismic activity is one of the signs volcanologists look for when evaluating whether the volcano is about to become active or not.

Volcanologists monitor deformation of the surface of a volcano. Steam and other gasses heated by rising magma cause the volcano to swell. Rising magma can press against the magma plug in the crater of the volcano, causing the plug to bulge. Volcanologists climb down into the crater to place and retrieve monitoring equipment that records deformation of the plug.

False color infrared image of Mount St. Helens the day before it erupted. The blue area is the snowcap, red indicates heated areas of the volcano.

As an eruption draws nearer, gasses and steam may be released from the summit or flanks of the volcano. Rising magma heats water and gasses trapped in the rock and forces steam and gasses to the surface. The increased temperature of the volcano can also be detected and measured by infrared cameras either mounted on aircraft, of infrared imaging satellites. As the temperature of the volcano increases, the image becomes measurably brighter on the infrared pictures.

Volcanologists use these and other measurements to evaluate the likelihood of an eruption, the severity of the eruption if there is one, and the likely path of destruction. They also determine the kind of material most likely to be ejected from the cone. Some eruptions spew tons of ash into the air, choking nearby life and burying it in a thick layer of ash. Others eject fast or slow-moving lava down the face of the volcano, plowing barriers aside and igniting anything in its path. Still others, like Mount St. Helens, erupt so violently that the side of the mountain fails, and the mountain blasts enormous portions of itself into the air before collapsing on one or more sides.

Summary

The devastation that can be caused by a volcano and the difficulty in understanding such a long-lived feature compared to human lifetimes requires the application of science to provide warning of impending disaster. People living in the neighborhood of a volcano become inured to its occasional rumblings and ventings, ignoring the signs of impending disaster until it is too late. Scientists measure seismic events caused by movement of magma beneath the volcano, deformation of the volcano's surface, changes in steam or gas venting, and increased heat to predict the approach of an eruption.

Concept Reinforcement:

1. Why do people ignore a volcano's warning signs that it is preparing to erupt?

2. What measurements do volcanologists take to monitor a volcano's state?

3. What can volcanologists predict about an eruption, based on their measurements?

Chapter 12 – Preventing Catastrophes When Volcanoes Erupt

- Analyze how we can use science to predict volcanic eruptions, and prevent catastrophe

Introduction

Volcanoes can lie dormant for hundreds to tens of thousands of years, giving no sign of life, then suddenly awaken to cause massive damage and change the planet's climate. Volcanologists measure seismic events caused by movement of magma beneath the volcano, deformation of the volcano's surface, changes in steam or gas venting, and increased heat to predict the approach of an eruption. Volcanologists use these and other measurements to evaluate the likelihood of an eruption, the severity of the eruption if there is one, and the likely path of destruction.

Volcanologists also determine the kind of material most likely to be ejected from the cone. Some eruptions spew tons of ash into the air, choking nearby life and burying it in a thick layer of ash. Others eject fast or slow-moving lava down the face of the volcano, plowing barriers aside and igniting anything in its path. Still others, like Mount St. Helens, erupt so violently that the side of the mountain fails, and the mountain blasts enormous portions of itself into the air before collapsing on one or more sides.

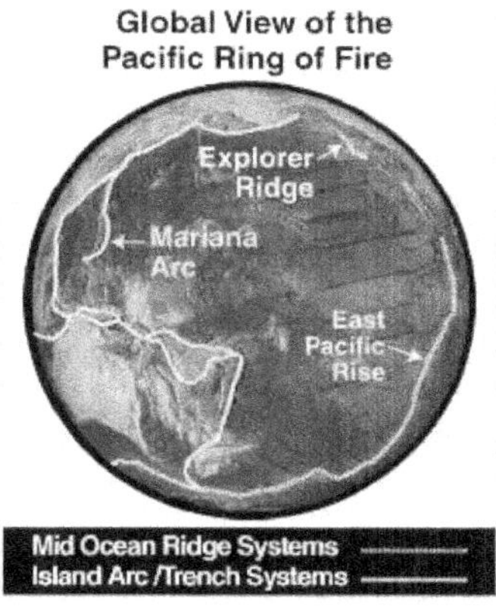

Avoiding catastrophe

Of course, the best way to avoid volcanic catastrophe is to avoid living in the vicinity of a volcano. However, the Pacific Ring of Fire includes vast stretches of the coasts of the United States, Japan, China, Australia, and numerous Pacific Islands. In fact, many of the islands in the Pacific are the result of undersea volcanoes growing until they emerged from the ocean to form dry land. The Hawaiian Islands, while not part of the Ring, are the result of volcanic activity caused by a hot spot, an intraplate volcanic zone caused by a mantle plume.

"

The United States' Geological Survey (USGS), part of the Department of the Interior, offers a Volcano Hazards Program to help local leaders develop emergency response plans in the event of a volcanic eruption. Plans include emergency responders' drills for fire, police, and medical first responders, close interaction with the media in the event of an emergency, and education of the population through field trips and classroom visits by USGS personnel and local officials.

Land use planning should take into consideration the likely path of destruction in the event of an eruption. Structures should not be built in areas likely to be overflowed by lava. Barriers may be positioned to attempt to direct the flow of lava away from areas of concern. Such barriers must not be viewed as foolproof. With temperatures ranging from 700° to 1,600° C, almost anything in the path of a lava flow can melt or ignite. The amount of lava likely to be extruded is also a concern. Magma flows have ranged historically from 0.5 cubic meters per second (m^3/s) to an estimated 5,000 m^3/s. That is comparable to a large wheeled garbage can-full of lava per second at the 0.5 m^3/s rate, to a container 12 stories high and 120 feet long on each side every second at 5,000 m^3/s. While a reinforced concrete barrier might deflect a flow of 0.5 m^3/s, nothing is going to stop a flow of 5,000 m^3/s. Ashfall is a major concern when the primary ejecta from the volcano is ash. Ash completely buried the city of Pompeii in 79 C.E. The ash is blazing hot, and is capable of starting fires where it lands.

Ashfall after the eruption of Mount Pinatubo in 1991

Because of the destructive force of a volcano and the unlikelihood of stopping the effluvia from the volcano, an evacuation plan must be in place for any population center near a volcano. Routes must be mapped out that will not become closed by the eruption, and residents should be given as much warning as possible.

Summary

Volcanoes can lie dormant for hundreds to tens of thousands of years, giving no sign of life, then suddenly awaken to cause massive damage and change the planet's climate. Volcanologists measure seismic events caused by movement of magma beneath the volcano, deformation of the volcano's surface, changes in steam or gas venting, and increased heat to predict the approach of an eruption. Local authorities should have evacuation plans in place, have prepared first responders with emergency drills, and plan to use land in the path of volcanic effluvium in ways that will not compromise the economic recovery of the area after an eruption.

1. Why is it important to know the type of ejecta that may come from an erupting volcano?

2. Why do people live near volcanoes?

3. What can people do to prepare for an eruption?

Chapter 13 – Understanding Landslides, Mudflows, and Lahars

Chapter Objective:

- Explain how scientists measure, monitor and evaluate landslides, mudflows, and lahars

Introduction

Landslides, mudflows, and lahars differ from the other phenomena concerning movement of the Earth we have investigated thus far. Earthquakes, tsunamis, and volcanoes are the result of movement far beneath the surface of the Earth at the boundary between the crust and mantle. Landslides, mudflows, and lahars are movements of the uppermost layers of the Earth's crust; the soil and underlying rock that forms the soil.

Landslides are the result of soil and rock moving down slope under the effect of gravity, usually as a result of instability of the slope. Slope instability can be a result of erosion undermining the lower portions of the slope, saturation of the soil with water, thereby increasing the mass of the soil so that it overcomes the frictional force holding the soil in place, earthquakes, or volcanic eruptions. Loss of vegetation holding the soil in place can also cause landslides.

Mudflows and lahars are movements caused by liquefaction of earth by water. Mudflows are movement of surface materials caused by intense rainfall, sudden overflowing of lakes, or bursting of dams. Mudflows are extremely fast and can rapidly bury whatever is in their paths. Lahars are made from volcanic material such as volcanic ash or lava mixed with water. The water source for a lahar is typically from a stream, river, glaciers, or lake water. Lahars move quickly and are searingly hot.

Lahar flowing down Mount St. Helens in March 1982

Monitoring movement of the surface layers of the Earth is accomplished using geodetic measurements including geodetic markers that are placed at specific locations. Small bronze markers are placed at intervals all across the US with precise measurements of the latitude, longitude, and elevation of the marker. Periodically, technicians recheck the location of the markers and report any movement. Global Positioning Satellite (GPS) location data is also used to determine the exact position of a GPS monitoring device. Some of these devices are capable of reporting their location and changes in their location in real time.

Members of the US Army Corps of Engineers evaluate a slope in El Salvador for landslide potential

A non-geodetic device used to study the movement of the Earth's surface is a Slope Stability Radar (SSR). SSR allows for real time monitoring of the slope with submillimeter accuracy. If a slope begins to move, its rate of deformation will increase for a short period before it fails and begins to slide. Another non-geodetic tool used to monitor slope movement is a beam inclinometer. A beam inclinometer measures the flexing of a solid beam due to changes in load. As the slope settles, the beam load increases and so does its flexion. The flexion of the beam can be monitored robotically, and reported via satellite or landline to scientists monitoring the slope.

Slope Stability Radar scanning a mine for settling before a collapse

The potential for landslides, mudflows, and lahars is due to a number of factors specific to each site and requires careful evaluation. The slope of the land required for a landslide may be no more than 10% in one area, but might be as high as 40% or more elsewhere. The soil type, water capacity and saturation, subsoil, and bedrock all affect how well the soil adheres to the slope. Vegetation can significantly improve the soil's ability to adhere to the slope by anchoring it in place with solid root structures that penetrate into the bedrock. Bare or rocky soils are more likely to move. The potential for landslides, mudflows, and lahars increases in earthquake-prone areas. Lahars cannot form without volcanic activity in a region. Civil and environmental engineers take precise measurements of all of these factors, and develop mathematical models from which they predict the probability of landslides, mudflows, and lahars.

Summary

Landslides, mudflows, and lahars are movements of the uppermost layers of the Earth's crust; the soil and underlying rock that forms the soil. Landslides are the result of soil and rock moving down a slope under the effect of gravity, usually as a result of instability of the slope. Mudflows and lahars are movements caused by liquefaction of earth by water. Mudflows are movement of surface materials caused by intense rainfall, sudden overflowing of lakes, or bursting of dams. Mudflows are extremely fast and can rapidly bury whatever is in their paths. Lahars are made from volcanic material such as volcanic ash or lava mixed with water. Geodetic and non-geodetic methods are used to measure and monitor movement of surface materials on a slope. Civil and environmental engineers take precise measurements of a number of site-specific factors and develop mathematical models from which they predict the probability of landslides, mudflows, and lahars.

Concept Reinforcement:

1. What is the difference between a landslide and a mudflow or lahar?

2. What are the primary methods of measuring and monitoring landslides, mudflows, and lahars?

3. What are some of the variables engineers must consider when evaluating the potential for landslides, mudflows, and lahars?

Chapter 14 – Preventing Landslides, Mudflows, and Lahars

Chapter Objective:

- Understand the role science plays in preventing landslides, mudflows, and lahars

Introduction

Landslides, mudflows, and lahars are movements of the uppermost layers of the Earth's crust; the soil and underlying rock that forms the soil. Landslides are the result of soil and rock moving down slope under the effect of gravity, usually as a result of instability of the slope. Slope instability can be a result of erosion undermining the lower portions of the slope, saturation of the soil with water, thereby increasing the mass of the soil so that it overcomes the frictional force holding the soil in place, earthquakes, or volcanic eruptions. Loss of vegetation holding the soil in place can also cause landslides. Knowledge of the underlying causes of landslides, mudflows, and lahars can help scientists propose preventative measures that local authorities can take to reduce property damage and loss of life.

Modeling risk

Scientists use Geographic Information Systems (GIS) software to model the topography of a particular slope. They are able to overlay types of vegetation, soil type, soil moisture and water capacity information, and land disturbance zones such as roads which contribute to landslide risk because of vibration created by passing traffic. When these and other variables are entered, the computer's algorithms produce colored maps indicating the level of landslide or mudslide risk in a particular area. Scientists can then make recommendations about whether or not a proposed road or landuse should be permitted in an area because of its effect on local landslide or mudslide risk. In many cases, a proposed road can be relocated to a safer region, or the landslide-prone surface can be bridged instead of placing a roadbed on it.

Prevention measures that can lessen the risk of slides:
These are structures designed to catch debris flow from a slide

Once areas prone to landslide or mudslide have been identified, preventive measures can be taken to reduce the chance of a slide. Because soil moisture contributes to landslides, one of the methods of preventing landslides is to provide subsurface drainage systems to remove excess water. Some surfaces that are prone to landslide can be stripped so there is nothing left to slide. Piles, walls, cribs, or toe supports can be placed in positions to support loose earth and prevent it from slipping. Loose material can be solidified by chemical treatment including spraying of dilute cement to bond loose particles together.

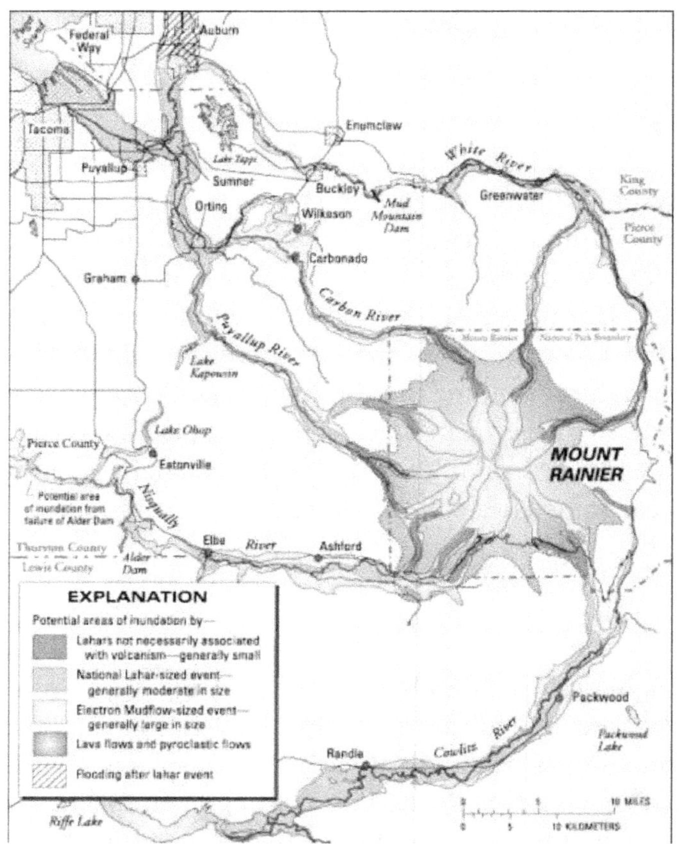

Lahar inundation model, Mount Rainier. Note the lahar paths

Lahars are significantly more difficult to control. Because of their volcanic nature, they happen very quickly and flow rapidly. Millions of cubic meters can be released almost instantly if a volcanic crater lake wall is ruptured by an eruption of the volcano. Early warning systems can provide residents an opportunity to flee, but residents must be educated as to the danger and provided information about where to go in an emergency. Some authorities have advocated building dams, but dams must be able to withstand the powerful forces unleashed during an eruption while holding back a sudden torrent. Dams also suffer from their trapping of sediments. Lahars are basically rivers of superheated mud with the consistency of concrete which will quickly bury a dam with sediment. Channels can be blasted into the side of the volcano to channel lahars away from populated areas. However as is the case with dams, sedimentation may quickly fill the channels.

Summary

Landslides, mudflows, and lahars are movements of the uppermost layers of the Earth's crust; the soil and underlying rock that forms the soil. Knowledge of the underlying causes of landslides, mudflows, and lahars can help scientists propose preventative measures local authorities can take to reduce property damage and loss of life. Using computer models, scientists can predict areas at high risk for landslides, mudflows, and lahars. Mitigation projects such as drainage installations, surface stripping, piles, walls, cribs, toe supports, or chemical solidification can be conducted to reduce the danger posed by landslides and mudslides. Lahars are significantly more difficult to control. Early warning systems, dams, and channels blasted into the volcano's surface may provide residents with some measure of safety, but the most important factor is preparedness.

Concept Reinforcement:

1. What are the factors that contribute to landslides and mudslides?

2. How can landslides and mudslides be prevented?

3. How can lahars be prevented?

Chapter 15 – Predicting Landslides, Mudflows, and Lahars

- Analyze how we can use science to predict landslides, mudflows, and lahars, and prevent catastrophe

Introduction

Landslide, mudslide, and lahar-prone areas are carefully monitored by government and university scientists around the world. The speed with which these disasters move and the abruptness of their onset shortens warning time for local residents. Scientists use a variety of monitoring devices to detect imminent collapse. They also design public awareness and education campaigns and materials to educate the local population and local officials about the dangers of landslides, mudflows, and lahars and what to do in an emergency.

Predicting failure

High accuracy GPS antenna used to measure earth subsidence

Failure of a slope resulting in landslides or mudslides is a process that gives short, but noticeable warnings. Global Positioning Satellite (GPS) location data is used to determine the exact position of GPS monitoring devices on such a slope. When these devices report changes in their location in real time, scientists examine the magnitude of the change and compare it to predictions based on complex computer models. When movement reaches a threshold value, an alert is broadcast to local authorities and residents.

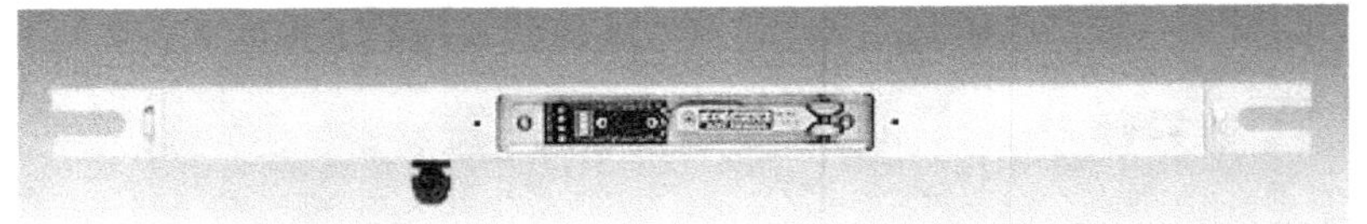

Slope Stability Radar (SSR) allows for real time monitoring of the slope with submillimeter accuracy. If a slope begins to move, its rate of deformation will increase for a short period before it fails and begins to slide. SSR is capable of scanning an entire slope face every few minutes, providing constant updates of surface conditions.

Beam inclinometer

Beam inclinometers, which measure the flexing of a solid beam due to changes in load, are another non-geodetic tool used to monitor slope movement. As the slope settles, the beam load increases and so does its flexion. The flexion of the beam can be monitored robotically, and reported via satellite or landline to scientists monitoring the slope. When the flexion exceeds specified limits, a slide is imminent and a warning is broadcast.

Geophones used to sense dam failure and lahar movement.

Lahars are different in that they are triggered by volcanic activity. Background seismic activity associated with a volcano can result in the failure of a dam holding back superheated water and ash, resulting in a lahar. Early warning systems for lahars include geophones which are capable of "hearing" the collapse of dams holding back volcanic lakes, water level monitors that alert when water levels drop suddenly, and buried tripwires that detect dam collapse. The speed with which lahars travel results in little warning time to residents. Residents and authorities must be well briefed on what to do. Action plans are drawn up and practiced by first responders so they are prepared in the event of a lahar.

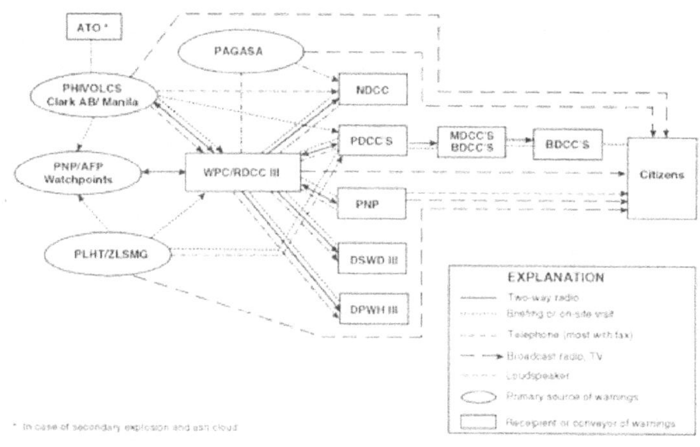

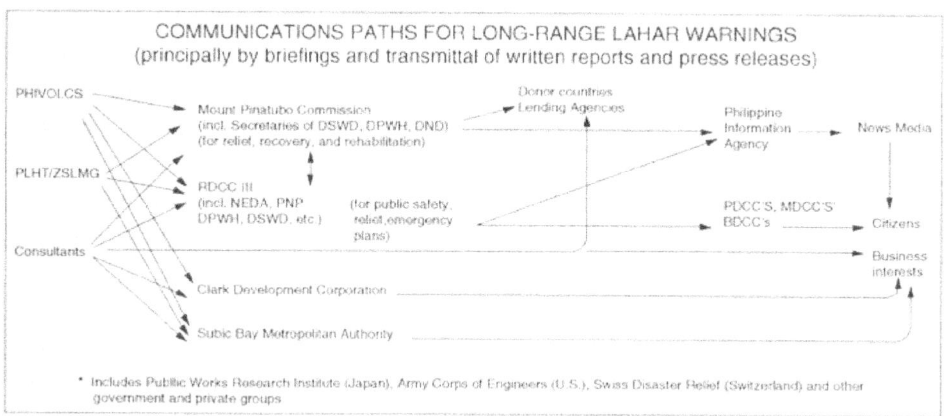

Response plan in case of lahar

Summary

Scientists use a variety of monitoring devices to detect imminent collapse of land surfaces that result in landslides, mudslides, or lahars. GPS monitoring devices, Slope Stability Radar, inclinometers, geophones, and tripwires are just a few of the tools scientists have at their disposal to predict and detect land surface failure. Scientists also design public awareness and education campaigns and materials to educate the local population and local officials about the dangers of landslides, mudflows, and lahars and what to do in an emergency.

Concept Reinforcement:

1. How does a GPS monitoring device warn of a landslide?

2. How does a beam inclinometer warn of an landslide?

3. How do geophones warn of a lahar?

Chapter 16 – Introduction to Hydrological Disasters/Climatic Disasters

Chapter Objective:

- Introduce the various hydrological and climatic disasters and investigate the science of these disasters

Introduction

Life exists on Earth because of the ready availability of liquid water. Before there was a high level of oxygen in the atmosphere there was life, and many species of bacteria thrive only in the absence of oxygen. Without water at the right times and in the correct measure, life ceases. Water moves over the planet in an endless cycle, called the Water Cycle. Water evaporates from the planet's surface into the atmosphere. Warm air is capable of holding greater quantities of water than cooler air. As the air cools, the water vapor condenses. When water droplets condense they form clouds. When enough water droplets are present, they collide and form droplets that are so large they fall from the sky as precipitation. The pattern of precipitation on the land dictates the type of plants and animals that can live in a given location. This pattern of precipitation can be disrupted, resulting in floods or droughts.

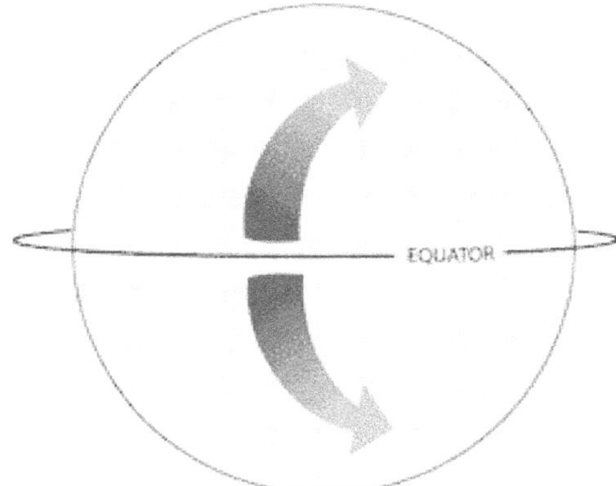

Movement of air over the planet as a result of heating and Coriolis forces.

The water vapor is transported around the planet via winds that result from the heating of the Earth's surface by the Sun and Coriolis forces generated by the rotation of the Earth. As the Sun heats the surface of the planet, the air above the surface absorbs some of that heat. Air near the poles is cooler than air over the equator. Air over water is heated more slowly than air over land because water absorbs more of the Sun's heat than land. Land reflects much of the Sun's energy back into the atmosphere above it. But water cools more slowly, too, so air above water is heated later into the night after the Sun has set, while air over land cools.

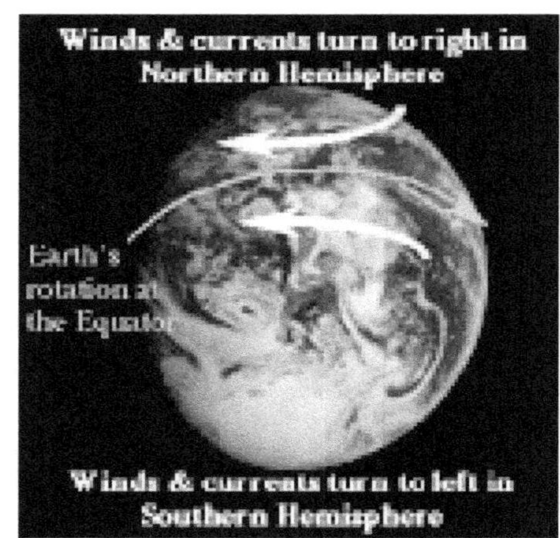

The heated air rises and the cooler air sinks causing vertical currents in the atmosphere. Air also moves from the equator toward the poles for the same reason. Cool air moves in to areas vacated by the rising warm air. As the planet rotates beneath the rising and falling air, it imparts a counterclockwise twist to the air in the Northern Hemisphere, and a clockwise twist to the air in the Southern hemisphere. These twisting forces are called Coriolis forces. Coriolis forces are very weak, but over vast distances can create weather systems of enor-mous power, of which the result is the hurricane, also called a typhoon or cyclone.

Hydrological and climatic disasters

Severe forms of precipitation such as hail, sleet, or blizzard snows are caused by collisions of air masses with very different temperatures and moisture levels. When very warm, moist air collides with very cool dry air, the warmer air is forced upward over the cooler air. As it rises, the warm air cools and the moisture condenses to fall a precipitation. The collision of the two air masses results in vortices which can touch down as tornados. Falling water may freeze as sleet or snow. In other cases, winds aloft may toss frozen pellets back up-wards where they collect more water and refreeze. If the process is repeated often enough, large hailstones can be formed.

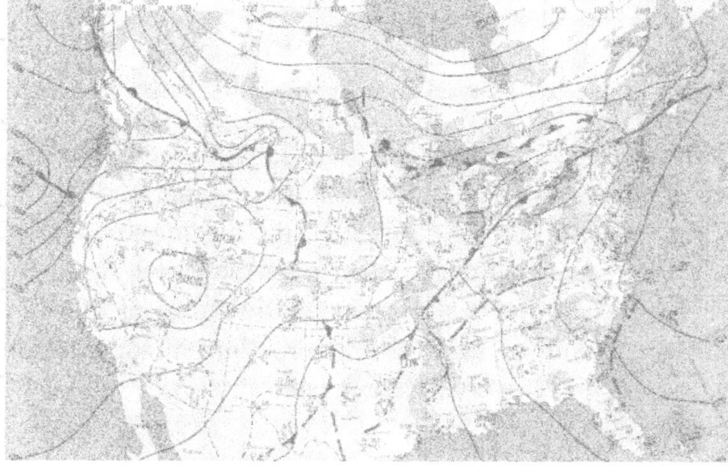

High and low-pressure systems with their rotation and temperature

Wildfires, hurricanes, and heat waves can result from excessive heating of the planet's surface. As the heat accumulates, the air over the land is forced upward. The rising air can push the Jet Stream, a high altitude wind that circles the planet near the poles at high speed. The Jet Stream can form ridges that prevent air masses from moving, or it can push them along more rapidly if they coincide with its path. A warm dry air mass can develop and be held in place over land, resulting in a heat wave. Heat waves dry the underlying country-side, making it prone to wildfires. When the vegetation becomes dry enough, it takes very little to spark a blaze that can destroy tens of thousands of acres of wilderness and any structures in its path. Hurricanes are similar in that they are warm air masses, but they form over warm waters and draw their heat from the water. They build strength because of the Coriolis forces acting upon them coupled with the continued input of warm, moist air from the warm waters of the equator.

Summary

Water supports life on Earth as no other element or compound can. Water is transported around the planet in the Water Cycle, a continuous process of evaporation and condensation, which results in precipitation. Precipitation can take many forms, depending upon the temperature in which it is formed. Winds, generated by the uneven heating of the planet's surface and the Coriolis force, move the water in the atmosphere from one region to an-other. Collisions between air masses of different temperatures result in water vapor in the warm air condensing and falling as precipitation. The greater the difference in temperature between the two air masses, the more likely the storm created will be violent, spawning sleet, hail, blizzards, or tornadoes. Wildfires, hurricanes, and heat waves can result from ex-cessive heating of the planet's surface. Air heated over land is dry, and results in heat waves and wildfires. Air heated over the oceans is moist, and generates hurricanes.

Concept Reinforcement:

1. What is the water cycle and why is it important to the plants and animals on the land?

2. How is wind generated?

3. How are hurricanes different from heat waves?

Chapter 17 – Understanding Floods

- Explain how scientists measure, monitor and evaluate floods

Introduction

Floods are caused by heavy precipitation, damming of running water, tsunamis, and storm surges generated by hurricanes as they approach land and make landfall. In this chapter, we will focus on floods due to precipitation. Floods due to precipitation, including the melting of snowpack in the Mountain West and Northeastern US, are caused by the inability of the soil to absorb water. This is due to saturation or the soils inability to absorb water as rapidly as the water covers the soil. When this happens, water flows over the land to streams, rivers, lakes, and ponds. As their water level increases, they overflow their banks and cover the land with water in a flood.

Severe Flooding

Floods cause damage to property and loss of life. People can be carried away and drowned in rapid currents, struck by debris, electrocuted by downed power lines, or sucked into unseen drains beneath the surface. Property can be saturated with water, and be damaged by mold and mildew growth and contribute to the damage. Structures are weakened and undermined, or lifted off of foundations and carried away. Silt containing heavy metals, agricultural chemicals, untreated sewage, and other hazardous waste can be spread over small towns and blocks of large cities. The cost of cleaning up after a flood is extremely high. For these reasons, scientists measure, monitor, and evaluate the risk of flooding to provide adequate warning of impending high water.

Scientists measure floods using flood gauges. Flood gauges measure the height of the water in a river, stream, lake, or other body of water. When the height of the water reaches the height of the banks, flood stage is reached. The height of the water above flood stage indicates how much water is present, and how much of the surrounding countryside the water will cover.

Flood gauges also provide scientists with information about the flood crest, the highest water level that can be expected in a flood. As a flood develops and moves downstream, the crest of the flood moves with it. Scientists monitor the progress of a flood by monitoring the movement of the flood crest. The National Oceanic and Atmospheric Administration (NOAA, pronounced Noah) maintains 3780 flood gauges across the United States. Flood information can be obtained at any time on NOAA's website by checking the status of NOAA's flood gauges.

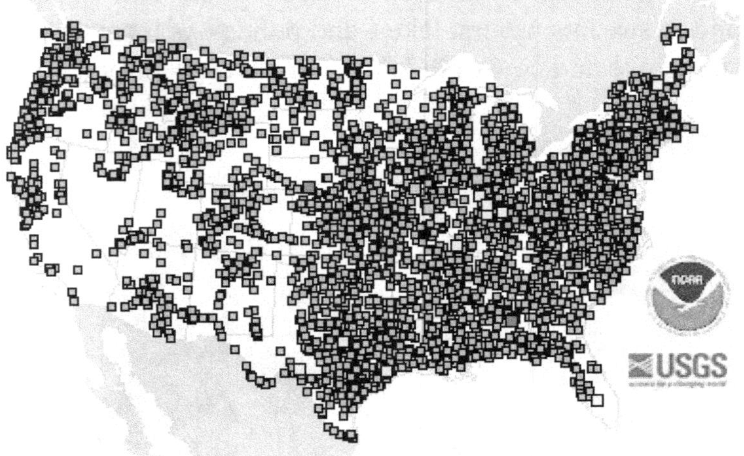

NOAA's flood gauge map. Colors other than green indicate flooding or impending flooding.

Floodwaters can contain high levels of bacteria and dissolved chemicals that are hazardous to human and animal health. Water chemists collect samples of floodwaters to examine the bacterial load and determine what hazardous chemicals may be present. Water samples can be tested for bacterial load by placing samples of the water on microbiological growth plates and incubating the plates overnight. Bacterial colonies will form on the plates and they can be counted. The more bacterial colonies there are, the higher the bacterial load. Waterborne bacteria can be examined under a microscope for classification, or their DNA can be collected and processed to determine which bacteria are present in the water.

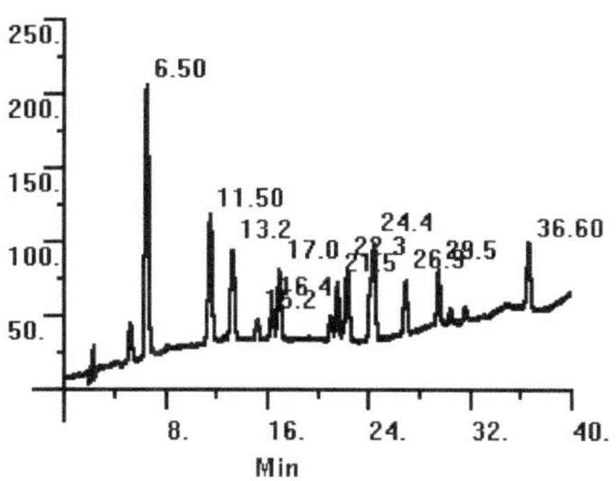

Results from a chromatographic analysis indicating the presence of a variety of chemicals.

Chemical analysis of the water for dissolved chemicals is typically conducted using chromatography (kro-mah-TAH-grah-fee). Chemicals are forced through a molecular sieve in a chromatograph (kro-MAT-oh-graf), and detected in a variety of ways as they pass through the sieve. Water chemists can determine the type and quantity of chemicals in the floodwater using specific detectors for suspected chemicals, and non-specific detectors for chemicals whose presence is not obvious.

Floods are evaluated by the amount of land they inundate and the damage they cause. Aerial imagery can easily depict the amount of land inundated. Radar images can determine the depth to which the land has been covered. Scientists are further interested in the amount of time required for floodwaters to recede. Floodwater recession can be affected by the slope of the land, soil saturation before the flood, and the local soil type. Damage reports are generated by civil and environmental engineers who estimate the structural integrity of structures, and environmental losses.

Summary

Floods due to precipitation are caused by the inability to the soil to absorb water. This is due to saturation or inability of the soil to absorb water as rapidly as the water covers the soil. Water flows over the land to streams, rivers, lakes, and ponds causing them to overflow their banks and cover the land with a flood. Scientists measure and monitor floods using flood gauges. Scientists monitor the progress of a flood by monitoring the movement of the flood crest. Water chemists collect samples of floodwaters to examine the bacterial load and determine what hazardous chemicals may be present. Floods are further evaluated by the amount of land they inundate and the damage they cause. Damage reports are generated by civil and environmental engineers who estimate the structural integrity of structures, and environmental losses.

Concept Reinforcement:

1. How do scientists measure and monitor a flood?

2. How do scientists determine what hazards are carried in the water?

3. What factors affect the rate of flood water recession?

Chapter 18 – Predicting Floods

Chapter Objective:

* Analyze how we can use science to predict floods, and prevent catastrophe

Introduction

Floods due to precipitation, including the melting of snowpack in the Mountain West and Northeastern US, are caused by the inability to the soil to absorb water due either to saturation or inability of the soil to absorb water as rapidly as the water covers the soil. When this happens, water flows over the land to streams, rivers, lakes, and ponds. As their water level increases, they overflow their banks and cover the land with water in a flood.

Predicting floods

Long-term flood predictions

Meteorologists predict floods for an upcoming year, season, month, week, day, even hours. They use a variety of data to predict impending floods. Long-term forecasts for flooding utilize sophisticated computer models that account for climate indicators.

El Niño, above, and La Niña, below. Notice the large warm water indicated by the white and red region to the west of South America during the El Niño event. Notice also the large, cool waters indicated by purple and blue during the La Niña event.

El Niño or La Niña conditions in the Pacific Ocean are measured using infrared satellite imagery that records the temperature of the waters off the coasts of Peru and Ecuador. El Niño, the boy child, is so named because it usually begins in December near Christmas time. Temperatures in the waters off the coasts of Peru and Ecuador increase. This increase warms and moistens the air above, changing wind patterns and increasing rainfall in southern California, the American southwest, and the American Midwest, among other places.

La Niña, the opposite of El Niño, creates cooler, drier conditions in the Midwestern US, dry conditions across the southern and southwestern US, and increased precipitation in the northern California mountains, the Pacific northwest, and the northern Rockies. Both systems can cause flooding, but each induces flooding in different regions of the country.

Scientists monitor snowpack in the Rocky Mountains and Coastal Range to estimate the amount of runoff to be anticipated during the spring and summer melts. Large snowpack coupled with rapid increases in temperature can result in floods because of the speed with which the snowpack melts and the inability of the soil to absorb all of the water.

Hurricane season predictions are an important part of long-term flood forecasts. Hurricanes dump torrential rains on large swaths of the southern United States. The rainfall totals can rapidly saturate the ground, making further water absorption impossible. Continued rainfall results in flooding as streams and rivers overflow their banks. Predicting where, when, and how often hurricanes can be expected can provide officials with time to plan for flood mitigation.

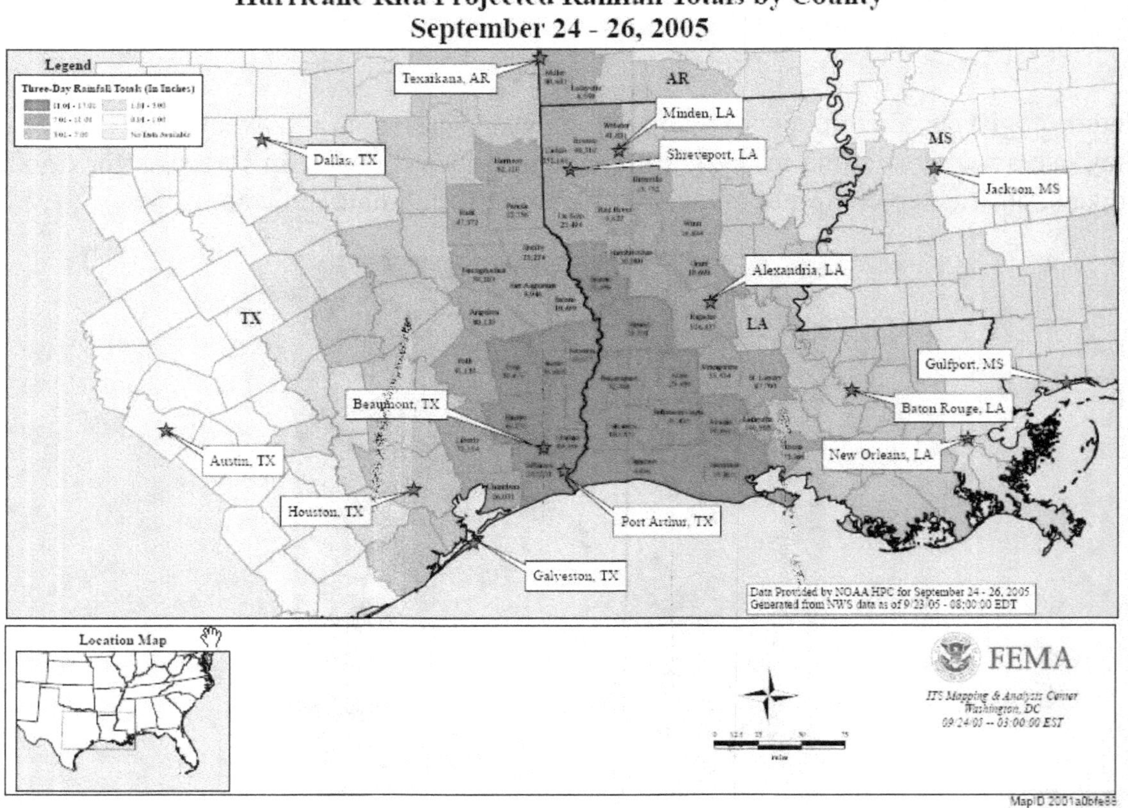

Rainfall total predictions for Hurricane Rita in September 2005 used by the Federal Emergency Management Agency (FEMA) to plan for emergency response to flooding.

Long-term flood predictions are used by emergency preparedness organizations to plan for upcoming flood seasons, budget for supplies and salaries, and strengthen flood mitigation and community outreach programs long before flooding occurs.

Aerial image of soil saturation taken by a NOAA reconnaissance aircraft prior to the arrival of a major storm system in central Texas in 2007. The image was vital to flood preparations for the region.

Nearer term flood forecasts are more dependent upon rainfall measurements, speed with which a weather system is moving and its direction, soil saturation, and water levels in local bodies of water. Rain gauges measure rainfall amounts, satellite images and ground-based sensory stations measure the speed of passing of storm systems, and an estimate of the amount of water reaching the ground during the period of time the storm will be preset can be made. Combined with soil saturation data and topographical information, predictions can be made for flood warnings to be issued.

Flood gauge on the Tar River in North Carolina.

Once flooding has begun, scientists track the flood's progress using flood gauges located on rivers, streams, lakes, and floodplains. Floods build over time until they reach their highest water level, or crest. Scientists track the movement of the flood crest as it progresses downstream to provide warnings to local officials and inform the community when the greatest danger has passed.

Summary

Meteorologists make both long-term and near-term flood predictions to reduce the loss of life and property damage done by floods. Meteorologists use satellite imagery to track ocean temperatures, wind patterns, snow pack in the mountains, and hurricane season pre-dictions to make long range predictions about the likelihood of flooding so that emergency planners can prepare for the upcoming year. When flooding is imminent, meteorologists measure rainfall, soil saturation, storm movement, and riverine water levels to provide warning to communities in flood-prone areas to prepare for flooding or to evacuate.

Concept Reinforcement:

1. What long-term flooding patterns would be expected during an El Niño year?

2. What long-term flooding patterns would be expected during a year with higher than normal predictions of hurricane activity?

3. What are the factors that affect near term flood risk?

Chapter 19 – Understanding Droughts

*   Explain how scientists measure, monitor and evaluate droughts

Introduction

A drought is a prolonged period of reduced water supply to a region. Typically, the lowered water supply is due to reduced precipitation. Occasionally, drought can result from changes in the plant cover or tillage practices on the soil, which reduce its ability to capture and retain water. Droughts are a normal part of climatic and weather patterns, but a prolonged drought can have severe economic consequences. Droughts in developing countries can cause widespread hunger and famine. Dry soils are also more prone to erosion from wind. During the Dust Bowl of the 1930s, topsoil from Texas, Oklahoma, Kansas, and Colorado farms blew across the country to be deposited in the Atlantic Ocean.

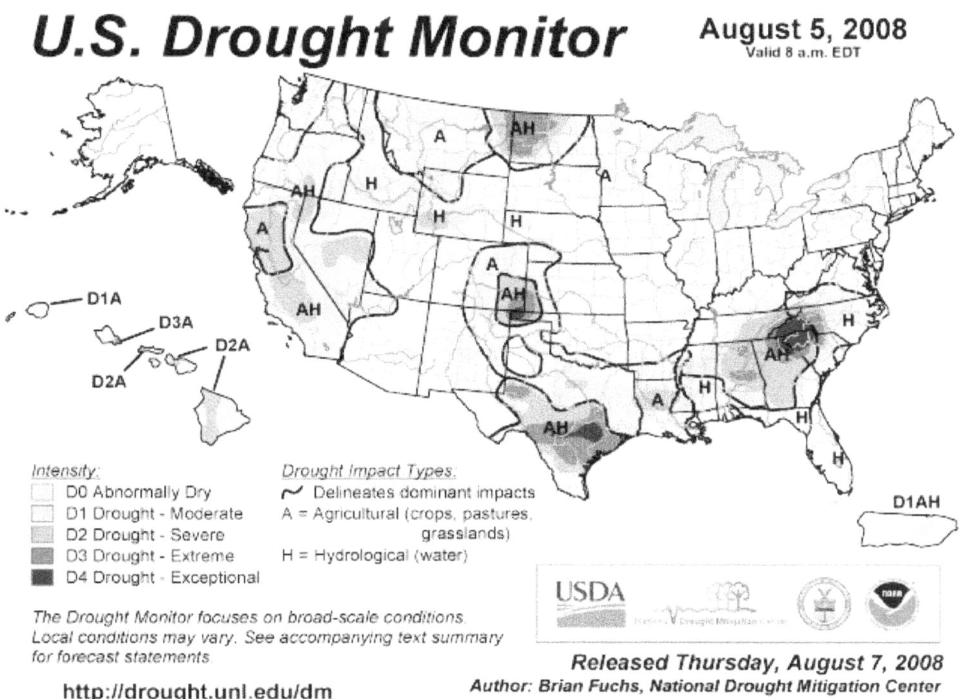

Droughts have been called the silent disaster. Droughts progress slowly, so there is little to no drama as in the case of floods or hurricanes. But droughts cause more economic damage over longer time frames than most other natural disasters. The National Oceanic and Atmospheric Agency (NOAA) estimates drought losses to be $6 to $8 billion annually. Because of the silent nature of a drought and its high cost, NOAA scientists and scientists at the US Department of Agriculture's (USDA) Soil Conservation Services (SCS) carefully monitor drought conditions across the US. In fact, current climate models predict an increase in the frequency and severity of droughts in the US.

Meteorologists and agronomists monitor drought using a variety of data. They also measure, monitor, and evaluate drought conditions and probability over long-term and near-term time horizons.

Precipitation data is one measure used in drought tracking. Most droughts in the US are a result of declining precipitation. Meteorologists track precipitation and compare previous years' precipitation totals and patterns with current year totals and patterns to estimate whether a drought is approaching, present, expanding, or relieved.

Meteorologists also track changes in the surface temperature of Pacific waters off the western coasts of Peru and Ecuador. El Niño or La Niña conditions in the Pacific Ocean can change drought patterns in the US significantly. Increasing global temperatures are predicted to increase drought in some regions of the country, but bring increased moisture and drought relief to others. Current climate models are not sufficiently sophisticated to make accurate predictions on any but the broadest of scales.

Soil temperature monitoring as part of soil moisture monitoring in the Owyhee River Basin, Idaho.

Soil moisture is a critical indicator of drought conditions. The primary concern regarding drought is its effect on crops and livestock. If the soil holds sufficient moisture, crops will thrive even if there has been little rainfall. However dry soils will not support plant life. Soil moisture is affected by evaporation rate. Soil moisture evaporation rate is affected in turn by plant cover, air temperature, soil temperature, and relative humidity. Estimates of these factors are made using standard thermometers, black body thermometers, wet bulb thermometers, soil temperature gauges, and direct measurements of plant cover. Water runoff is the final variable considered in determining soil moisture. Depending upon the soil type and slope of the land, high runoff can indicate either soil saturation or soil that is unable to absorb moisture before it runs off.

Droughts are typically accompanied by higher than normal temperatures. These higher temperatures increase evaporative losses, increase plant transpiration, and increase the ability of the air to hold water rather than release it as precipitation. Meteorologists track frontal boundaries and the Jet Stream to estimate how long a localized drought will last and when it can be expected to end.

Summary

Droughts have been called the silent disaster. Droughts progress slowly, so there is little to no drama as in the case of floods or hurricanes. But droughts cause more economic damage over longer time frames than most other natural disasters. A drought can be caused by declining precipitation due to El Niño or La Niña conditions in the Pacific Ocean, climate change, and stationary air masses that contain little water. Meteorologist and agronomists measure, monitor, and evaluate droughts using satellite imagery, precipitation data, temperature data, and soil type and slope data. Drought conditions are predicted to increase in the United States; bad news for the billions around the world who depend upon American agriculture to sustain them and prevent hunger.

Concept Reinforcement:

1. What is a drought?

2. What are the factors affecting a drought?

3. What do meteorologists and agronomists measure to track a drought?

Chapter 20 – Predicting Droughts

Chapter Objective:

- Analyze how we can use science to predict droughts, and prevent catastrophe

Introduction

Droughts have been called the silent disaster. A drought progresses slowly, so there is little to no drama as in the case of floods or hurricanes. But a drought causes more economic damage over longer time frames than most other natural disasters, $6 to $8 billion per year in the US alone. A drought often goes almost unnoticed until long after it has begun to affect crop and livestock production and cause widespread economic damage. For these reasons, scientists work to predict droughts to initiate drought mitigation measures to reduce the damage they cause not only to agriculture, but to wild life as well.

Drought prediction

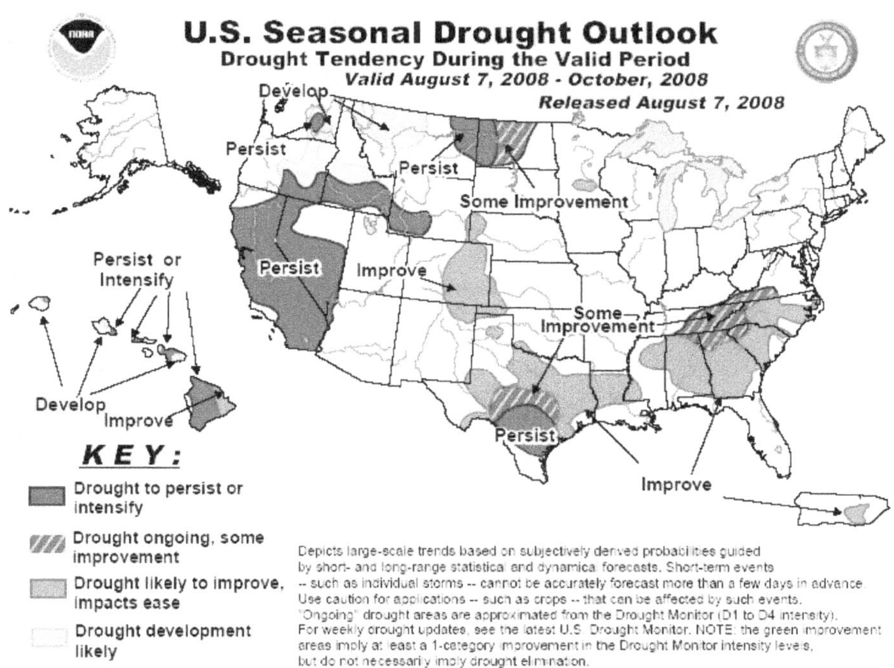

Meteorologists and agronomists working for the National Oceanic andAtmospheric Agency (NOAA) and the US Department of Agriculture's (USDA) Soil Conservation Service (SCS) use sophisticated computer-based climate models to forecast drought for the upcoming year. Parameters included in NOAA and SCS climate models include El Niño or La Niña conditions in the Pacific Ocean, annual precipitation data, Jet Stream analysis, hurricane forecasts, soil moisture levels, vegetative soil cover, snow pack volume and conditions, stream flow data, and topography. NOAA forecasters will be the first to admit that the complexity of climate modeling and climatologists' incomplete understanding of how the variables contributing to climate interact, make accurate drought forecasting nearly impossible. However, drought response and mitigation efforts by local and federal authorities is usually poor, at best, and any preparative information NOAA can provide to help mitigate the effects of prolonged drought should help emergency response planners be better prepared to recognize and respond to a drought.

Drought mitigation

In order to mitigate the effects of a drought, it is important to first understand where a drought has its impacts. In California, for example, approximately 85% of the water used in the state is used for agricultural production. Only 15% of the total water use for the state of California is for industrial use followed by residential use. Drought mitigation efforts should start with agricultural water conservation plans rather than the more typical municipal conservation planning conducted to mitigate drought.

Fish sampling during a drought in North Carolina.

Drought impacts fish and wildlife, tourism, agriculture, industry, health, wildfire danger and the ability to combat wildfires, energy production, health, municipalities and their water supplies, and residential users. Each of these impacted activities must be considered in a functional drought mitigation plan. State and local governments must have plans in place to resolve conflicting water use priorities. For example, fish and wildlife require water, and some must be reserved for their use. But powerful agricultural and industrial lobbies pressure legislators to raid water reserved for fish and wildlife for their needs instead.

Plans should include:

- triggers for drought declaration

- early warning of approaching drought

- limits on urban development to match water availability

- low interest loans for farmers and small businesses

- development of reservoirs and emergency water supplies

- public awareness and conservation campaigns

- improvement of water conveyance systems (repair of leaky pipes, and broken pumps

- voluntary restrictions on irrigation

- changes in water rights and the right to sell water

- suspension of water use permits in threatened watersheds

- establishment of hay hotlines and emergency livestock watering locations

- special permits for farm irrigation

- drought recovery funds

Summary

Droughts have been called the silent disaster. A drought progresses slowly, so there is little to no drama as in the case of floods or hurricanes. Scientists predict drought conditions using sophisticated computer-based climate models to forecast droughts for the upcoming year. However, drought models are not particularly accurate. Planning for droughts requires officials to be aware of the impacts of a drought. Understanding the impacts of a drought in their locality helps state and local authorities develop plans to reduce these impacts.

Concept Reinforcement:

1. What are the variables considered in drought prediction models?

2. What are the economic and other activities impacted by droughts?

3. How can state and local officials resolve conflicts over water use during a drought?

Chapter 21 – Understanding Thunderstorms and Hailstorms

- Explain how scientists measure, monitor and evaluate severe thunderstorms and hailstorms

Introduction

Severe thunderstorms are responsible for property damage and loss of lives due to high winds, hail, and lightning. Severe thunderstorms are also capable of causing localized flooding in low-lying areas, and flash floods in mountain streams. Flash floods in dry streambeds can appear suddenly and without warning even though the rain may have fallen many miles away in nearby mountains. Scientists measure, monitor, and evaluate severe thunderstorms and hailstorms to learn more about their causes and to better predict where and when they will develop.

Thunderstorm Development

Thunderstorms can develop in several ways, but they all have a common thread: warm moist air rises and cools causing the water vapor in the air to condense to form clouds. Thunderstorms can form when warm and cold fronts collide, when warm moist air is pushed up and over mountains, or simply from convection heating moist air over land causing the air to rise.

As the water vapor in the air condenses, each ice crystal that forms releases a small amount of heat. At such high altitudes, the water will freeze rather than form a liquid water droplet. The heat released when the water vapor condenses and freezes is added to the surrounding air, causing updrafts that force the air higher where it can continue to cool. Eventually the rising air, and the cloud that has formed because of the condensation of water vapor reach a layer of air, the tropopause, that caps its upward movement and the top of the cloud spreads downwind in an anvil shape called a thunderhead.

Developing Thunderstorm

As the ice crystals accumulate and grow, they begin to fall toward the ground as precipitation. The falling precipitation creates downward air movements. The cooler air at the top of the cloud also begins to sink back toward the ground where it can be reheated. These movements of air create downdrafts. The updrafts and downdrafts can create a conveyer system thrusting more warm, moist air upward to create more condensation. The up- and downdrafts also create winds as the thunderstorm develops. Another cause of wind in a thunderstorm is the creation of an area of low pressure directly beneath the developing clouds. As the warm air rises, the air pressure beneath falls. Surrounding higher pressure air rushes into the low-pressure region creating winds that move toward the approaching storm and feeding more warm, moist air into the clouds.

Hail formation

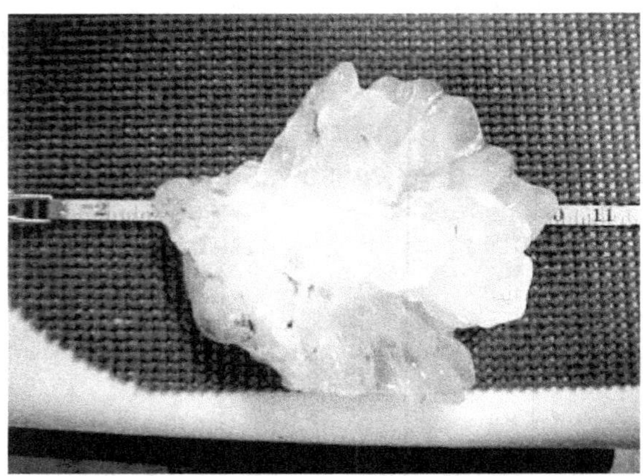

Hailstone

When the condensed ice crystals have grown large enough, they begin to fall. As they fall they thaw if the air is warm enough and fall as rain. If not, they fall as snow. If the updrafts within the cloud are strong enough, the ice crystals may fall far enough to partially thaw and then be hurled back aloft, accumulating more water and refreezing to form hail. More violent thunderstorms generate larger hail because of the strength of their updrafts, which cycle growing hailstones back upwards more frequently than less powerful storms. The evidence of hailstone formation can be seen by cutting a hailstone in half and examining the growth rings. Each time the hailstone returned to the upper levels of the storm to accumulate more water, a new ring is formed. The largest hailstone on record to fall in the US measured 7 inches across and 18.75 inches in circumference.

Lightning

Lightning is the characteristic hallmark of a thunderstorm. Lightning is an electrical current through the air that carries charge between the clouds and the ground beneath. Lightning heats its surroundings to over 10,000°C, twice as hot as the surface of the Sun. The almost instantaneous heating of the air propagates a shockwave that is heard as thunder. Sound travels much more slowly than light, so the flash of a lightning bolt always preceded the sound of the thunder. Sound travels approximately 1 mile every 5 seconds, so by counting the number of seconds between the observation of a flash of lightning and the arrival of the thunderclap, the distance from the bolt of lightning can be roughly estimated.

Scientists do not fully understand how lightning is generated, but they have two possible explanations, or *hypotheses*. However, in both cases, electrical induction and the violent winds inside a thundercloud are responsible for the creation of the electrical charge that results in lightning. Water droplets and ice crystals collide with one another in the cloud as they are tossed about by the winds inside the cloud. When they collide, electrons can be passed from the lighter particles to the heavier ones. The heavier particles fall toward the bottom of the cloud, causing a build-up of negative charge at the bottom and a positive charge near the top. The negative charge near the bottom of the cloud induces the develop-ment of a positive charge in the ground below. When the positive and negative charges be-come large enough, a bolt of lightning arcs between the cloud and the ground. Negatively charged particles stream downward to be met by upwardly streaming positive particles. When they meet, a bolt of lightning is discharged from the base of the cloud. Lightning strikes generate low frequency radio waves that can be detected, counted, and located using radio detectors.

Measuring, monitoring, and evaluating severe thunderstorms and hailstorms

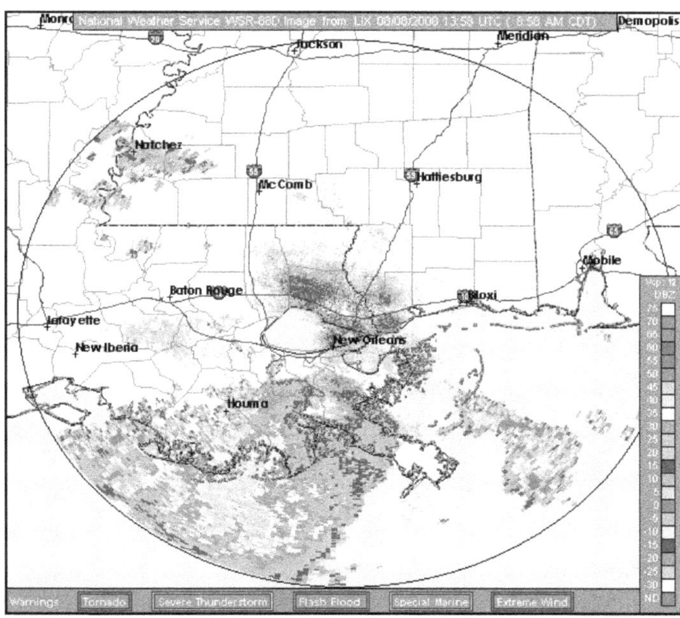

Doppler weather radar image

Meteorologists measure, monitor, and evaluate severe thunderstorms and hailstorms using a variety of tools. One of the most commonly used tools is Doppler radar. Doppler radar uses radar to measure the movement of water within the clouds to estimate the severity of the storm. The size of the particles and the speed with which they move can be determined and used to estimate the amount of water in the cloud and the speed of the winds within the cloud. Wind shear, which can generate tornados, is also measured using Doppler radar. Anemometers measure wind speeds, rain gauges measure the amount of precipitation that falls from the clouds, hailstones are measured, lightning strikes are recorded using radio detectors, and satellite imagery is used to measure cloud size, depth, temperature, move-ment, and lightning generation upward into the stratosphere. Meteorologists combine all of this information to create a final picture of the size of the thunderstorm, how long it is likely to last, its direction of travel, and its severity.

Summary

Thunderstorms are immensely powerful atmospheric disturbances that generate wind including tornadoes, precipitation in the form of rain, snow, or hail, and lightning. The damage caused by thunderstorms includes flooding, wind damage, lightning damage, and hail damage. Thunderstorms are caused by rising warm moist air, which cools as it rises. Water vapor condenses and forms ice crystals which fall as precipitation. Meteorologists measure, monitor, and evaluate severe thunderstorms and hailstorms using Doppler radar, aeromometers, precipitation gauges, radio detectors, and satellite imagery.

Concept Reinforcement:

1. What causes the winds inside a developing thundercloud?

2. How is hail formed?

3. How are lightning strikes monitored?

Chapter 22 – Predicting Thunderstorms and Hailstorms

- Analyze how we can use science to predict severe thunderstorms and hailstorms, and prevent catastrophe

Introduction

Thunderstorms are immensely powerful atmospheric disturbances that generate wind including tornados, precipitation in the form of rain, snow, or hail, and lightning. The damage caused by thunderstorms includes flooding, wind damage, lightning damage, and hail damage. Thunderstorms are caused by rising warm moist air, which cools as it rises. Water vapor condenses and forms ice crystals which fall as precipitation. Meteorologists predict the development and movements of severe thunderstorms and hailstorms using air pressure measurements, Doppler radar, aeromometers, precipitation gauges, radio detectors, and satellite imagery. The National Weather Service issues storm watches and warnings based on these measurements so local residents can be prepared.

Prediction of a thunderstorm

Meteorologists monitor severe thunderstorms and hailstorms using a variety of tools. One of the most commonly used tools is Doppler radar. Doppler radar uses radar to measure the movement of water within the clouds to estimate the severity of the storm. The size of the particles and the speed with which they move can be determined and used to estimate the amount of water in the cloud and the speed of the winds within the cloud. Wind shear, which can generate tornadoes, is also measured using Doppler radar. When high wind shear is observed, tornado watches and warnings are issued for localities in the path of the storm.

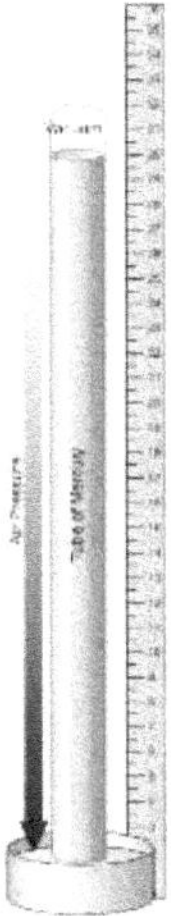

Mercury barometer. Notice the open grey tube into which mercury would have been poured. Such an apparatus is not considered safe today because of mercury vapor escaping into the air from the pool.

As we noted in the previous chapter, the air movement within a thunderstorm causes the atmospheric pressure in the region of the storm to decrease. Meteorologists measure atmospheric pressure at weather monitoring stations scattered across the country using a barometer. Early barometers were glass tubes closed at one end. Each tube was filled with enough mercury to create a column about 30 inches high. The open end of the mercury-filled tube was then inserted into a pool of mercury. When the air pressure on the mercury increased, the column of mercury inside the tuberose. When the air pressure decreased, the column fell. Anaeroid barometers are barometers that use a small chamber that can be compressed by high atmospheric pressure or decompressed low atmospheric pressure. Anaeroid barometers are more commonly used in modern meteorology. However, atmospheric pressure is still reported in inches or millimeters of mercury in the US.

The size of the drop in atmospheric pressure is an important indicator of the potential power of a developing thunderstorm. Very low atmospheric pressures are closely associated with more powerful storms, with higher winds, damaging hail, and more lightning. Likewise, frontal boundaries with very different pressures generate more powerful storms.

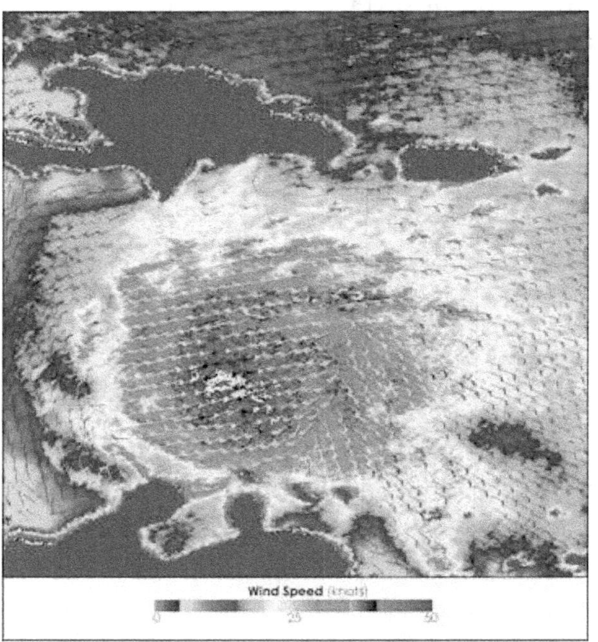

False color satellite image of a storm

Satellite imagery is used to measure cloud size, depth, temperature, movement, and lightning generation upward into the stratosphere. The temperature of the clouds at different levels indicates the amount of energy a developing storm possesses. Recall that updraft and downdrafts result from warm and cool air masses rising and falling. The greater the temperature differences within the cloud's layers, the greater the power of the up- and downdrafts. Powerful updrafts suspend ice crystals in the cloud for longer periods creating larger hailstones. Powerful downdrafts play a role in spawning tornadoes. The more powerful the downdrafts, the greater the risk of tornadoes and the more powerful those tornadoes are likely to be.

Lightning strikes are recorded using radio detectors and satellite images. Lightning is generated by collisions among water droplets and ice crystals in the cloud. More violent storms generate more and more powerful lightning. Meteorologists observe the frequency and magnitude of lightning strikes to determine storm strength, and to issue severe storm warnings.

Preventing catastrophe

Meteorologists observe the signs of a developing thunderstorm and predict its potential to cause damage. When a severe thunderstorm is predicted, a severe thunderstorm watch or warning is issued by the National Weather Service (NWS). A watch indicates conditions are right for the formation of a large thunderstorm within the next 24 hours. A warning indicates a thunderstorm has been spotted and is expected to move into the area soon. Citizens are advised to seek cover and remain indoors. Low-lying areas are issued flood watches or warnings, and people are advised to stay away.

Warnings such as these give people time to move vehicles and other outdoor items under cover to avoid hail damage. Local authorities are placed on alert. Utility companies alert repair crews to stand by in case of downed power lines. Recovery efforts can be coordi-nated, and losses can be reduced. In some cases, such as a hurricane or tropical storm, there may be a period of calm as the eye of the storm passes over an area. Meteorologists warn residents not to be fooled, and that the storm will return shortly as the eye moves past and the wind and rain return.

Summary

Thunderstorms are immensely powerful atmospheric disturbances that generate wind including tornadoes, precipitation in the form of rain, snow, or hail, and lightning. The damage caused by thunderstorms includes flooding, wind damage, lightning damage, and hail damage. Meteorologists predict the development and movements of severe thunderstorms and hailstorms using air pressure measurements, Doppler radar, aeronometers, precipitation gauges, radio detectors, and satellite imagery. Changes in atmospheric pressure are a primary indicator of the potential power of an approaching storm. Lower atmospheric pressure is associated with more powerful damaging storms. The National Weather Service issues storm watches and warnings based on these measurements so local residents can be prepared.

Concept Reinforcement:

1. Why is atmospheric pressure an important indicator of storm strength?

2. How is atmospheric pressure measured?

3. What is the difference between a thunderstorm watch and a thunderstorm warning?

Chapter 23 – Understanding Tornadoes

Chapter Objective:

- Explain how scientists measure, monitor and evaluate tornadoes

Introduction

Tornadoes are rotating columns of air that form within supercell thunderstorms. A tornado is created when horizontally rotating columns of air, that form before the thunderstorm, are lifted vertically by rising warm moist air. Tornadoes can remain on the ground for over 30 miles and leave a path of destruction over one mile wide. Tornado winds can exceed 250 mph, but more typically average less than 110 mph. However 110 mph is the uppermost boundary wind speed for a category 2 hurricane, so an average tornado is a very powerful wind. Approximately 90% of presidential disaster area designations are weather related, and tornadoes make up a large proportion of those disasters. Meteorologists carefully monitor weather patterns for the possibility of tornado development and issue tornado watches and warnings to local residents so they can prepare for potentially dangerous winds and take shelter.

Measuring and evaluating tornadoes

Tornadoes in the US are measured on the Enhanced Fujita Scale (EF) based on the Fujita scale developed by Dr. Tetsuya Fujita at the University of Chicago. The EF assesses the damage done by the tornado and estimates wind speeds based on the damage done. Tornadoes are assigned an EF number from 0 to 5, with EF 0 tornadoes being relatively weak, to EF 5 tornadoes being the strongest ever recorded. There have been no EF 5 tornadoes recorded since the National Weather Service (NWS) began using the EF system. The EF scale uses 28 damage indicators that rate wind speeds based on damage to vegetation and buildings.

FUJITA SCALE			DERIVED EF SCALE		OPERATIONAL EF SCALE	
F Number	Fastest 1/4-mile (mph)	3 Second Gust (mph)	EF Number	3 Second Gust (mph)	EF Number	3 Second Gust (mph)
0	40-72	45-78	0	65-85	0	65-85
1	73-112	79-117	1	86-109	1	86-110
2	113-157	118-161	2	110-137	2	111-135
3	158-207	162-209	3	138-167	3	136-165
4	208-260	210-261	4	168-199	4	166-200
5	261-318	262-317	5	200-234	5	Over 200

Monitoring tornadoes

Meteorologists rely on Doppler radar to measure the speed of winds approaching and receding from the radar station to predict cyclonic activity within storm cells. If the movement becomes sufficiently rapid, a tornado watch is issued. However, tornado spotting and monitoring is still a decidedly low-tech operation. Doppler radar only allows meteorologists to anticipate a tornado. They cannot actually spot and monitor tornados using radar alone. The NWS trains everyday citizens as well as law enforcement and emergency response personnel to visually detect and report tornados. There are over 230,000 trained tornado spotters in the US.

Tornado with wall cloud.

Tornado spotters look to the rear of the storm to determine if there is a significant updraft. If so, they also look for a rotating wall cloud, indicative of rotating air within the supercell thunderstorm. If a clear area appears near the rotating wall cloud a tornado is imminent. The clear area is formed by a downdraft of cool air. If the downdraft of cool air balances the updraft of warm air, a funnel cloud may appear. A funnel cloud is a funnel shaped region of rotating air that creates a cloud by condensing water. Funnel clouds are the final indicator that a tornado is imminent, and may shortly touch down as a tornado.

GOES satellite moisture image.

Tornadoes can be monitored once they have been confirmed by tornado spotters using both Doppler radar and GOES satellites. GOES satellites are geostationary satellites that can monitor movement of warm and cool air masses and water vapor in the atmosphere. Warm moist air is critical for the formation of supercell thunderstorms and tornadoes. Meteorologists and atmospheric scientists can monitor severe weather as it happens using imagery from the GOES satellites.

Summary

Tornadoes are created when horizontally rotating columns of air, that form before the thunderstorm, are lifted vertically by rising warm moist air. Tornadoes in the US are measured on the Enhanced Fujita Scale (EF). The EF assesses the damage done by the tornado and estimates wind speeds based on the damage done. Meteorologists rely on Doppler radar and GOES satellite imagery to predict cyclonic activity within storm cells. Over 230,000 everyday citizens, law enforcement, and emergency response personnel are trained by the NWS to visually detect and report tornadoes.

Concept Reinforcement:

1. What is the Enhanced Fujita Scale and how does it assess tornadoes?

2. How does the NWS detect and monitor tornadoes?

3. What are the signs of an impending tornado?

Chapter 24 – Understanding Cyclonic Storms

- Explain how scientists measure, monitor and evaluate cyclonic storms

Introduction

Cyclonic storms are tremendous storms that develop around low-pressure disturbances in the atmosphere. They form over the warm waters of the tropical oceans as high heat and humidity cause the air in the region to expand and rise, creating a low-pressure region. Continued heating and addition of moisture generate circulating winds around the low-pressure system. Given sufficient heat and moisture, a cyclonic storm is born. Cyclonic storms in the Northern Hemisphere rotate counterclockwise, while cyclonic storms in the Southern Hemisphere rotate clockwise due to the Coriolis force generated by the rotation of the Earth.

Evaluating cyclonic storms

Cyclonic storms are given a variety of names based on their location and strength. For convenience, this article will use the designations commonly used by the United States. Cyclonic storms can be tropical depressions, tropical storms, and hurricanes.

Cyclonic storms are evaluated based on the strength of their winds using the Beaufort scale. The Beaufort scale was originally developed in 1805 and was based on the effects of the winds on sails. The scale was changed with the advent of steam-powered ships to the effects of the wind on the ocean and surface objects after landfall. The Beaufort scale ranges from 1 to 17, but 13 to 17 were added in 1946 and are not used in the US. Level 12 of the Beaufort scale is equivalent to a category 1 hurricane. Once winds reach Level 12 of the Beaufort scale, the Saffir-Simpson Hurricane Scale (SSHS) is used. The SSHS uses categories 1 through 5 to evaluate the strength of hurricane winds.

Cyclonic storms are categorized by their maximum sustained winds. Maximum sustained winds are defined by the National Weather Service (NWS) as the average wind speed measured at 10 meters above the surface for 1 minute. The international standard is similar, except that it uses the average wind speed over a 10-minute period. For this reason, NWS wind speed values are higher for the same strength storm.

Tropical depressions have maximum sustained winds of up to 38 mph. Tropical storms' maximum sustained winds range from 39 to 73 mph. Hurricanes have maximum sustained winds of at least 74 mph. Hurricanes are further categorized on the SSHS scale with category (see table).

Safir -Simpson Hurricane Scale

Category	Wind speed
1	74-95
2	96-110
3	111-130
4	131-155
5	> 155

Measuring cyclonic storms

Hurricane hunter aircraft flying out of Pensacola, FL for the National Weather Service.

Cyclonic storms are formed far out at sea where there are few, if any, permanent weather monitoring stations. Developing storms are detected and measured by satellite imagery, long range radar, weather buoys, ships and aircraft, and mobile weather stations designed to withstand the forces of hurricanes. When a storm is detected, reconnaissance aircraft are deployed to the site. They fly into the storm, taking measurements of wind speed and direction, atmospheric pressure, air and surface water temperatures, and precipitation. With advances in technology, unmanned aerial vehicles (UAVs) have been used with greater frequency to measure cyclonic storms' characteristics. Storm speed is measured using satellite imagery.

Color-enhanced satellite image of Hurricane Andrew, August 1992.

Cyclonic storms are monitored using satellite imagery when they are far out at sea. Satellite images are updated every 15 to 30 minutes. GOES satellites are geostationary satellites that can monitor movement of warm and cool air masses and water vapor in the atmosphere. Lower altitude NOAA satellites in polar orbits pass over the same portion of the Earth every 12 hours, and can view clouds and surface conditions during daylight conditions. The Defense Meteorological Satellite Program (DMSP) has the highest resolution imaging equipment available and has the capability to "see" in the visible light range at night.

As a storm system approaches land, Doppler radar stations can take frequent, every few minutes, images of cyclonic storms. Doppler radar is especially useful in measuring precipitation, wind speed and direction, and storm path.

Summary

Cyclonic storms are tremendous storms that develop around low-pressure disturbances in the atmosphere. They form over the warm waters of the tropical oceans as high heat and humidity cause the air in the region to expand and rise, creating a low-pressure region. Cyclonic storms are evaluated based on the strength of their winds using the Beaufort scale. Once winds reach Level 12 of the Beaufort scale, the Saffir-Simpson Hurricane Scale (SSHS) is used. The SSHS uses categories 1 through 5 to evaluate the strength of hurricane winds. Developing storms are detected by satellite imagery, long-range radar, weather buoys, ships and aircraft, and mobile weather stations designed to withstand the forces of hurricanes. When a storm is detected, reconnaissance aircraft are deployed to the site. Cyclonic storms are monitored using satellite imagery when they are far out at sea. As a storm system approaches land, Doppler radar stations can take frequent, every few minutes, images of cyclonic storms.

Concept Reinforcement:

1. What is the Beaufort scale and how is it used to measure cyclonic storms?

2. How are cyclonic storms measured?

3. How are cyclonic storms monitored?

Chapter 25 – Predicting Cyclonic Storms

- Analyze how we can use science to predict cyclonic storms, and prevent catastrophe

Introduction

Cyclonic storms are tremendous storms that develop around low-pressure disturbances in the atmosphere. They form over the warm waters of the tropical oceans as high heat and humidity cause the air in the region to expand and rise, creating a low-pressure region. Continued heating and addition of moisture generate circulating winds around the low-pressure system. Given sufficient heat and moisture, a cyclonic storm is born. Cyclonic storms generate high winds, torrential rains, severe lightning, and spawn tornados. Their potential to cause property damage and loss of life makes them objects of concern to emergency preparedness planners, and scientists have developed methods of predicting their strength, movement, and eventual landfall.

Predicting cyclonic storms

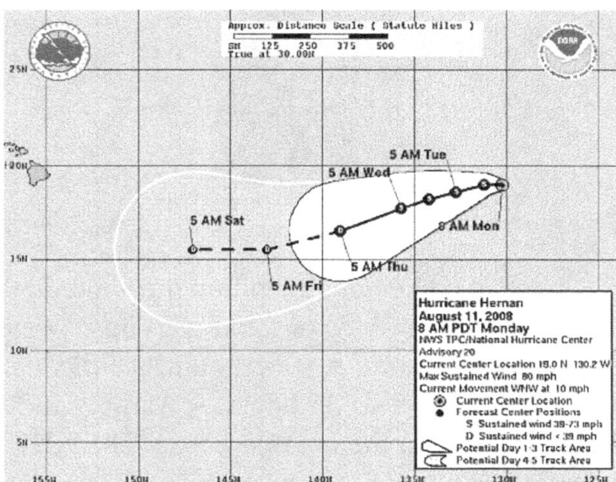

Atmospheric scientists and meteorologists predict cyclonic storm intensity and path. Each prediction requires a different set of measurements.

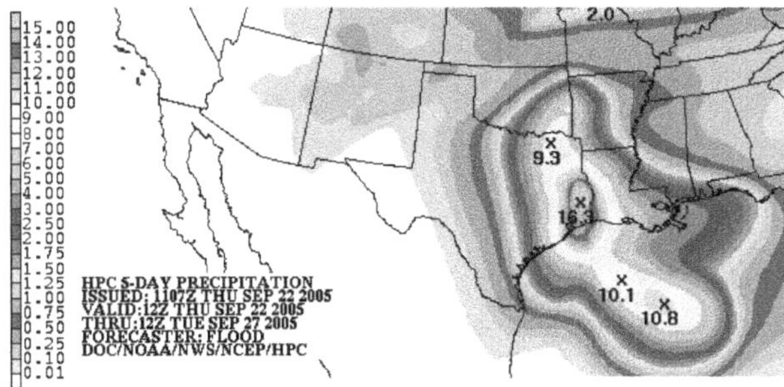

Rainfall prediction map for Hurricane Rita, September 2005.

Predicting the path of an approaching storm involves the use of supercomputers and computer models that incorporate the principles of fluid dynamics and thermodynamics from physics. The atmosphere is essentially a fluid surrounding a solid core. By measuring the pressure of the atmosphere at varying locations, air temperature, and wind movement at various altitudes, the direction and speed of a storm can be estimated. The National Oceanic and Atmospheric Administration (NOAA) uses a program called the Global Forecast System (GFS), which is updated every 6 hours. It predicts weather out to 384 hours, or 16 days. While it is fairly accurate for the first 7 days, forecasts beyond that time are not reliable. GFS is used by NOAA and National Weather Service (NWS) meteorologists to predict the path of cyclonic storms and their likely landfall locations. All GFS data is available free of charge to the public on the internet by law.

The intensity of a storm is much more difficult to predict. Meteorologists do not fully understand the dynamics occurring within a cyclonic storm. Factors affecting the strength of a cyclonic storm include heat of the surface waters, relative humidity, wind shear at various levels of the atmosphere, and the temperature difference between the upper and lower atmosphere. How changes in any one of these factors affect cyclonic storm formation and strengthening and the magnitude of their effects are not clear.

Preventing catastrophe

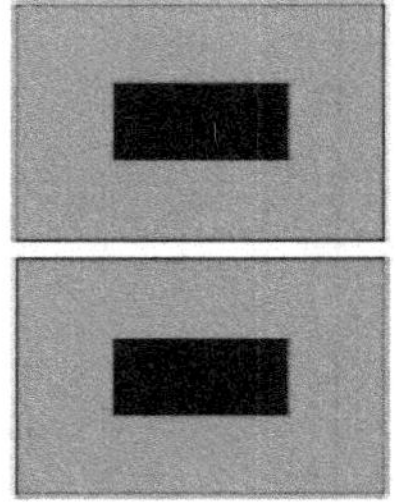

Hurricane warning flags warn ships of an approaching hurricane.

If a cyclonic storm is predicted to make landfall within the United States, the National Hurricane Center (NHC) issues a series of watches and warnings. Watches and warnings are issued for tropical storms and hurricanes. A watch indicates that a cyclonic storm poses a possible threat to a region within the next 36 hours. A warning indicates a cyclonic storm is expected to affect the region within the next 24 hours. The NHC also issues inland advisories warning inland residents of approaching high winds, torrential rains, and potential flooding.

Preparedness is the key to preventing catastrophe during cyclonic storms.

Cyclonic storms are regular events that will occur in certain regions of the country, especially the coasts of the Gulf of Mexico and Atlantic. Preparedness is the key to mitigating the damage of cyclonic storms. Weather specialists issue warnings that permit local authorities to plan for local evacuations, prepositioning of emergency supplies, and movement of recovery personnel including utility crews and possibly the National Guard near the area the storm will affect.

Building codes in regions prone to cyclonic storms can be strengthened, requiring builders to strengthen structures against high wind damage and water damage. Because flooding and storm surge often cause as much or more damage than the winds, building codes and property insurance regulations should include consideration of potential storm caused flood damage. Residents should be educated about what to do in the event of a storm, especially if they choose to remain and ride out the storm. Power and water are almost certain to be lost, and automatic generators can electrocute utility crews after the emergency is past if power generated by a resident flows back up the power lines. Crime and looting frequently precede and follow a severe storm, and residents should be aware of potential criminal activity in their area and the absence of local law enforcement officials who may have been evacuated and who will undoubtedly be stretched thin.

Summary

Cyclonic storms generate high winds, torrential rains, severe lightning, and spawn tornadoes. Their potential to cause property damage and loss of life makes them objects of concern to emergency preparedness planners. Scientists have developed methods of predicting a cyclone's strength, movement, and eventual landfall. The GFS computer model is used by NOAA and NWS meteorologists to predict the path of cyclonic storms and their likely landfall locations. The intensity of a storm is much more difficult to predict. Meteorologists do not fully understand the dynamics occurring within a cyclonic storm. The National Hurricane Center (NHC) issues a series of watches and warnings as a cyclonic storm ap-proaches landfall. Preparedness is the key to mitigating the damage of cyclonic storms.

Concept Reinforcement:

1. What data is used by GFS models to predict the path of a cyclonic storm?

2. What are the factors affecting the strength of a cyclonic storm?

3. What factors should be considered to be prepared for a cyclonic storm when it makes landfall?

Chapter 26 – Understanding Blizzards

Chapter Objective:

- Explain how scientists measure, monitor and evaluate blizzards

Introduction

A blizzard is a severe winter storm with high winds, low temperatures, and blowing snow that results from the collision of a high-pressure air mass with a low-pressure air mass. The warmer, moister air of the low-pressure system is chilled suddenly by the cooler high-pressure ridge and precipitation in the form of snow may fall as a result. There does not have to be any snow falling to create a blizzard. Snow picked up from the ground and blown around by the high winds of the storm can create blizzard conditions as well. The high difference in air pressure between the two masses is responsible for the high winds. The US National Weather Service (NWS) defines a blizzard as a winter storm having sustained winds of 35 mph or more, with visibility below ¼ mile due to blowing snow that lasts for at least 3 hours. There is no temperature requirement for a blizzard to meet the definition, but temperatures and wind chills are often extremely cold. Blizzards usually develop on the northwest side of a storm front where the air masses collide.

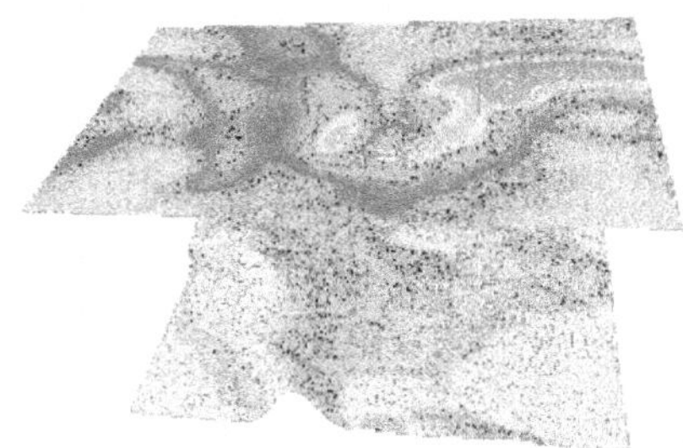

Computer generated image of the wind vectors and surface temperatures following the Blizzard of 1993, the worst to strike the US in over 100 years. Cool air can be seen flowing in to a region of low pressure (white arrows).

Measuring, monitoring and evaluating blizzards

Blizzards, like severe thunderstorms, are measured, monitored, and evaluated using atmospheric pressure measurements, Doppler weather radar, and GEOS weather satellites. Aeronometers measure wind speeds, and all-weather precipitation gauges measure the amount of precipitation that falls from the clouds. The most important consideration for blizzard formation is the atmospheric pressure, and the difference in pressure between the colliding air masses. Large differences in pressure cause air from areas of high pressure to rush in to the area of low pressure. This movement of high pressure, colder air creates the wind that causes blizzard conditions. Recall that precipitation is not necessary for a blizzard to develop. The movement of the low-pressure system across the continent is monitored using barometers in weather observation stations positioned throughout the country.

Blizzard

Doppler radar can be used to track the storm's progress. Wind speeds and precipitation can be estimated using Doppler radar as well. Doppler radar measures movement of objects such as air masses and precipitation by taking advantage of the Doppler Effect. Radar waves striking objects moving away from the receiver appear to be longer than radar waves striking objects moving toward the receiver. GEOS satellite images can provide visual images of cloud movements and infrared images of temperature gradients in clouds.

Reduced visibility due to blizzard snowfall.

When it does snow during a blizzard, the amount of snowfall is usually extreme. Snowfalls of several feet are not uncommon. High winds can pile snow into deep drifts, burying buildings. In especially severe conditions, a whiteout can occur. Visibility due to wind driven snow drops to near zero and it is easy to become disoriented.

Summary

A blizzard is a winter storm having sustained winds of 35 mph or more, with visibility below ¼ mile due to blowing snow, which lasts for at least 3 hours. A blizzard is a severe winter storm with high winds, low temperatures, and blowing snow that results from the collision of a high-pressure air mass with a low-pressure air mass. Blizzards are measured, monitored, and evaluated using atmospheric pressure measurements, Doppler weather radar, and GEOS weather satellites. When it does snow during a blizzard, snowfalls of several feet are not uncommon.

Concept Reinforcement:

1. What is a blizzard?

2. What is the most important factor in creating blizzard conditions, and how is it monitored?

3. How does Doppler radar work to measure, monitor, and evaluate blizzard conditions?

Chapter 27 – Predicting Blizzards

Chapter Objective:

- Analyze how we can use science to predict blizzards, and prevent catastrophe

Introduction

The US National Weather Service (NWS) defines a blizzard as a winter storm having sustained winds of 35 mph or more, with visibility below ¼ mile due to blowing snow that lasts for at least 3 hours. There is no temperature requirement for a blizzard to meet the definition, but temperatures and wind chills are often extremely cold.

Blizzard formation results from a collision between high- and low-pressure systems. The movement of these pressure systems is monitored using barometers in weather observation stations positioned throughout the country. Doppler radar can be used to track the storm's progress. Wind speeds and precipitation can be estimated using Doppler radar as well. GEOS satellite images can provide visual images of cloud movements and infrared images of temperature gradients in clouds.

Snowfall is not a requirement for blizzard conditions to exist. When it does snow during a blizzard, the amount of snowfall is usually extreme. Snowfalls of several feet are not uncommon. High winds can pile snow into deep drifts, burying buildings. In especially severe conditions, a whiteout can occur. Visibility due to wind driven snow drops to near zero and it is easy to become disoriented.

The NWS issues a blizzard watch when conditions are conducive to the development of a blizzard within the next 36 hours. A blizzard warning is issued when blizzard conditions are approaching. Watches and warnings are issued to allow residents time to prepare. When a blizzard approaches, residents should stay home or seek shelter. Driving can become extremely hazardous, as visibility is significantly reduced, and roads can become icy or drifted over with blowing snow.

Blizzards are very dangerous storms. There have been several instances of large numbers of people losing their lives because of disorientation in a whiteout. The so-called "Children's Blizzard" of 1888 caught many residents of the high plains of the US unprepared. It appeared without warning on a relatively warm day. Children were in barns or fields and became lost within 100 feet. Others were at school, many of them one-room schoolhouses. As a result, hundreds of lives were lost.

Downed power lines in Cleveland, OH after the Blizzard of 1913.

Wind-chill factors can be very low in a blizzard. Wind-chill is the perceived temperature felt on the skin because of the rapid conductance of heat away from the body by high winds. Wind-chill can cause frostbite on exposed skin, and hypothermia. Hypothermia is a lowering of the body's core temperature. When the temperature of the body drops, the individual becomes disoriented, confused, fatigued, begins to shiver uncontrollably, eventually enters a coma and dies.

Blizzards also can cause power outages due to strong winds, heavy snow, and icing of power lines or utility poles. Trees may ice up and break falling across and downing power lines as well. Water pipes can freeze and burst. During the blizzard, no water will be available. After the blizzard passes and the heat is restored, burst pipes may flood dwellings or roads. Fuel sources may be cut off as gas pumps and oil heaters may be jammed by ice crystals from incidental water vapor forming in the lines.

Summary

NWS meteorologists use barometers in weather observation stations, Doppler radar, and GEOS satellite images to predict blizzards. When a blizzard is imminent, NWS issues a blizzard watch when conditions are conducive to the development of a blizzard within the next 36 hours. A blizzard warning is issued when blizzard conditions are approaching. Watches and warnings are issued to allow residents time to prepare. When a blizzard approaches, residents should stay home or seek shelter. Blizzards can kill because of their low temperatures, high wind-chill factors, and blinding and disorienting snows. Blizzards also can cause power outages, burst water pipes, and eliminate fuel sources.

Concept Reinforcement:

1. What makes blizzards so dangerous?

2. What is the difference between a blizzard watch and a blizzard warning?

3. How do meteorologists predict blizzards?

Chapter 28 – Understanding Heat Waves

Chapter Objective:

- Explain how scientists measure, monitor and evaluate heat waves

Introduction

Summer in the United States is hot, and heat waves are seen nearly every summer in at least one region of the country. The National Weather Service (NWS) defines a heat wave as "a period of abnormally and uncomfortably hot and unusually humid weather. Typically, a heat wave lasts two or more days." Heat waves can damage property and important public infrastructure. Heat waves in Dallas, St Louis, New York, and Los Angeles have caused roads to buckle, power transformers to fail causing blackouts, and water mains to rupture. Increased demand for power to operate air conditioners can cause widespread blackouts. Heatwaves are often blamed for elevated fire risk and the advent of wildfires in drought-prone areas. Heat waves make wildfire more difficult to combat as well.

Heat waves are also deadly. Heat kills over 1,500 people in the US every year. On average, more people die from heat than hurricanes, tornadoes, lightning, and floods combined. Heatwaves also appear to kill people who might have lived had there been no heat wave. Deaths due to heart attacks and respiratory disease increase during heat waves. Records show that the number of deaths, especially in susceptible populations, increase significantly during the heat wave, then decline below normal for some time after the heat wave has passed. These records would appear to indicate that people who otherwise might have lived for some period of time were killed by the heat.

Heat waves evoke little in the way of public outcry for emergency preparedness because the damage property and take lives slowly and quietly. Most people simply retreat into their homes and wait them out.

Measuring, monitoring and evaluating heat waves

A heat wave is caused by a ridge of high pressure stalling over a region of the country for a period of days or weeks. In the western desert regions of the US, clear high-pressure air allows more solar radiation to reach the Earth to heat the land. In the eastern and south-eastern US, heat waves are caused by a high-pressure system stalling just off the coast. The clockwise rotation of the winds draw warm moist air from the Gulf of Mexico up and over the eastern seaboard creating a hot, humid heat wave.

Recall that the NWS defines a heat wave as a period of abnormally and uncomfortably hot and unusually humid weather that lasts two or more days. While true, this definition is not very helpful. Humidity increases the perceived temperature and decreases the body's ability to cool itself through sweat evaporation. As a result, the NWS created the Heat Index. The Heat Index is the apparent temperature as experienced by the body when the effect of the temperature and humidity are combined. Based on his research, Dr. Peter Robinson of the University of North Carolina at Chapel Hill has suggested that a heat wave should be defined as "a period of at least 48 hours during which neither the overnight low nor the daytime high Heat Index falls below the NWS heat stress thresholds (80° and 105°F, respectively)."

Heat Index values are developed for shade with a light breeze. Exposure to direct sunlight, hot dry winds, or other exacerbating conditions can increase the Heat Index for the immediate area by up to 15° F. The NWS issues a Heat Advisory within 12 hours of the onset of "a heat index of at least 105°F but less than 115°F for less than 3 hours per day, or nighttime lows above 80°F for 2 consecutive days."

Heat Index Chart. Follow the temperature column down to where it meets the humidity row across to determine the Heat Index for a given temperature and humidity. The shaded region above 105°F indicates a dangerous Heat Index that may cause severe heat disorders.

Temperature (°F)

Relative Humidity (%)	80	82	84	86	88	90	92	94	96	98	100	102	104	106	108	110
40	80	81	83	85	88	91	94	97	101	105	109	114	119	124	130	136
45	80	82	84	87	89	93	96	100	104	109	114	119	124	130	137	
50	81	83	85	88	91	95	99	103	108	113	118	124	131	137		
55	81	84	86	89	93	97	101	106	112	117	124	130	137			
60	82	84	88	91	95	100	105	110	116	123	129	137				
65	82	85	89	93	98	103	108	114	121	128	136					
70	83	86	90	95	100	105	112	119	126	134						
75	84	88	92	97	103	109	116	124	132							
80	84	89	94	100	106	113	121	129								
85	85	90	96	102	110	117	126	135								
90	86	91	98	105	113	122	131									
95	86	93	100	108	117	127										
100	87	95	103	112	121	132										

Likelihood of Heat Disorders with Prolonged Exposure or Strenuous Activity
Caution   Extreme Caution   Danger   Extreme Danger

The NWS uses sophisticated computer models to predict the probability of heat waves. I has developed the Heat Health Watch/Warning system to warn of excessive heat. The sys tem takes into account the occurrence of air masses that have historically produced danger ous heat and fatalities. The air masses are defined by a number of measurements including atmospheric pressure, temperature, winds, and season. The model can predict the expected length of a heat wave and its severity.

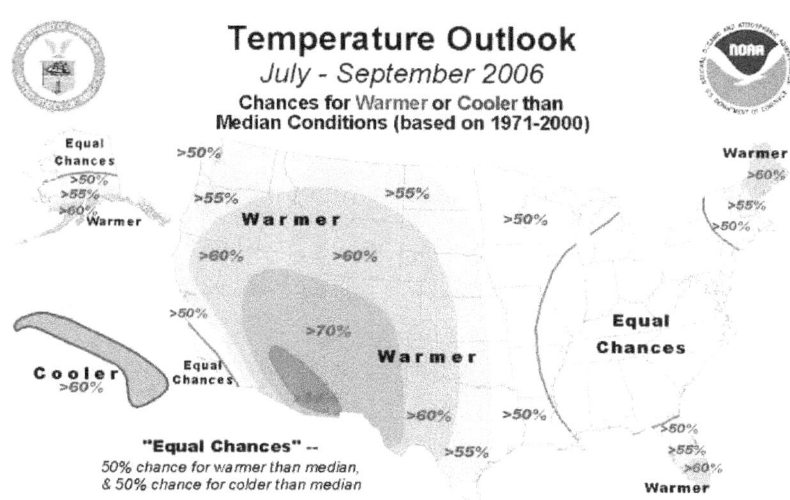

Summary

The National Weather Service (NWS) defines a heat wave as "a period of abnormally and uncomfortably hot and unusually humid weather. Typically, a heat wave lasts two or more days." Heat waves can damage property and important public infrastructure, and are responsible for more deaths than all other weather-related deaths except cold combined. A heat wave is caused by a ridge of high pressure stalling over a region of the country for a period of days or weeks. Humidity increases the perceived temperature and decreases the body's ability to cool itself through sweat evaporation. As a result, the NWS created the Heat Index, the apparent temperature as experienced by the body when the effect of the temperature and humidity are combined.

Concept Reinforcement:

1. What is a heat wave?

2. What is the Heat Index?

3. When is a Heat Advisory issued?

Chapter 29 – Understanding Wildfires

- Explain how scientists measure, monitor and evaluate bush fires

Introduction

Wildfires are becoming more common in the United States, especially in the Rocky Mountain region and the West Coast. Increasing global temperatures and prolonged drought have played a role in the onslaught of wildfires in the US. But the greatest contributor by far is the forest management practices of the past 60 years. Forest fire prevention and rapid response to extinguish forest fires coupled with decreased logging and grazing of National Forest Service (NFS) and Bureau of Land Management (BLM) lands have created a buildup of tree populations and underbrush that serves to weaken trees and increase dry fuel available of wildfire to burn. The result has been larger, hotter, more severe wildfires than at any time in US history, a situation unlikely to change any time soon.

Measuring, monitoring and evaluating bush ires

Fire scientists use a variety of long- and short-range imagery to map fire locations, determine vegetative cover before and after a fire, determine fuel type, and measure topography. Satellite data from LANDSAT satellites is used to measure burn areas. Satellite photos from after the fire can be layered over topographical maps using Geographic Information System (GIS) software. The GIS software can calculate the size of the burn and displays the topography. Satellite images are also used to determine the loss of vegetation. LANDSAT satellite images can measure peak photosynthetic activity in an area. By comparing "peak green" from before the fire to "peak green" after the fire, scientists can estimate the amount of vegetation lost to the fire and regrowth, if any. These data are combined into tables and maps statistically summarizing the effects of the fire.

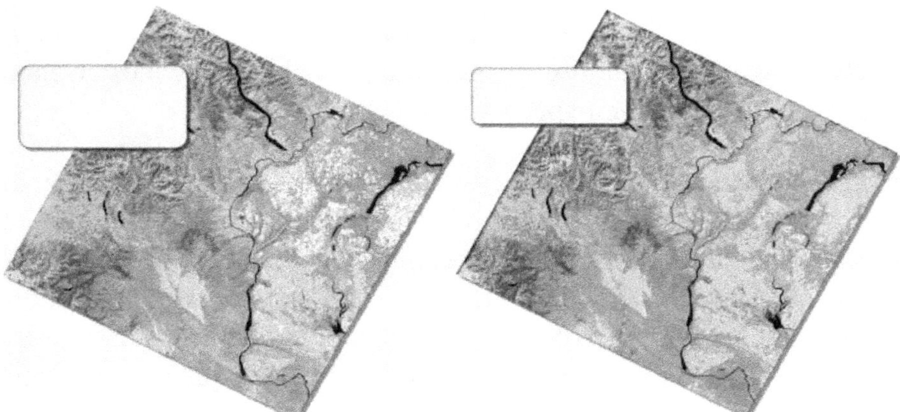

Pre- and post-fire satellite images. Notice the lighter colored are in the right-hand quadrant of the post-fire image denoting vegetation loss.

Satellite imagery and aerial reconnaissance photos are used to monitor the progress of wildfires that are still burning. Weather patterns are monitored for wind direction, changes in humidity, and rain chance to predict potential changes in the fire. Of particular importance are infrared images that show residual heat after a fire is declared out. Hotspots sometimes remain that require additional attention from firefighters.

San Diego wildfires destroy suburban homes.

Fire scientists also take land use patterns into consideration. Land use can be divided into urban, agricultural, suburban, forest, and grassland. Each land use pattern would be expected to have different burn characteristics. Urban areas would not be expected to suffer from considerable burning in the event of a wildfire as most of the structures are not in contact with wild lands. However suburban and agricultural lands can be severely affected by wildfires.

Forest and grassland each have different characteristics when burning and after they have burned. Grasslands burn quickly when dry, but usually recover quickly and do not generate intense heat. Forests, on the other hand, can burn at different levels and with different intensities. Fires on the ground level of a forest are relatively easy to combat, do little actual damage to the forest, and in most instances, are actually beneficial. They remove dead brush and create openings that allow new growth that provides increased food supplies to wildlife. Canopy fires, on the other hand, burn the tree tops, can develop intense heat which can sterilize the soil and slow regrowth, remove cover and wildlife habitat and feed, and spread rapidly by generating their own winds. Canopy fires are difficult to combat because of their speed and intensity.

Direct observation of the damage on the ground is used to measure, monitor, and evaluate the effects of a wildfire. Height and color of flames can give good approximations of the heat of the fire, its intensity, and its fuel source. Fire-generated winds can be followed visually by smoke, ash, and sparks lifted into the air. Spark direction and predicting the probability of sparks igniting additional blazes can be augmented by visual observation. Soil and vegetation moisture readings can be collected in advance of a fire to determine how dry the area is and how prone to ignition it is.

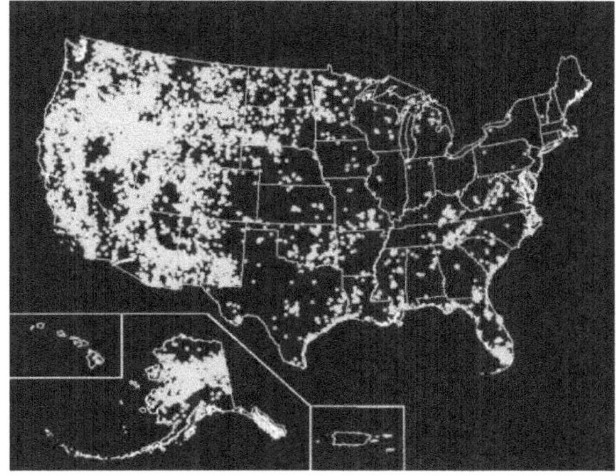

Wildfires of greater than 250 acres from 1980 – 2003.

The US Geological Survey (USGS) in cooperation with other federal and local agencies maintains maps of fires, their specifics, and dates for use by emergency planners.

Summary

Wildfires in the US destroy tens of thousands of acres every year. Their severity is growing every year. Scientists at the US Geological Survey, National Forest Service, Bureau of Land Management, and state and local scientists measure, monitor, and evaluate wildfires and their damage using satellite images, aerial reconnaissance photos, weather data, and observations on the ground. Improved understanding of previous wildfires enhances firefighters' ability to combat future blazes.

Concept Reinforcement:

1. What kinds of information do fire scientists use to compare pre- and post-fire damage?

2. How do scientists monitor fires as they burn?

3. How are ground observations used to measure, monitor, and evaluate fires?

Chapter 30 – Preventing Wild Fires

Chapter Objective:

- Analyze how we can use science to predict bush fires, and prevent catastrophe

Introduction

Wildfires are becoming more common in the United States, especially in the Rocky Mountain region and the West Coast. Increasing global temperatures and prolonged drought have played a role in the onslaught of wildfires in the US. But the greatest contributor by far is the forest management practices of the past 60 years. Forest fire prevention and rapid response to extinguish forest fires coupled with decreased logging and grazing of National Forest Service (NFS) and Bureau of Land Management (BLM) lands have created a buildup of tree populations and underbrush that serves to weaken trees and increase dry fuel available of wildfire to burn. The result has been larger, hotter, more severe wildfires than at any time in US history, a situation unlikely to change any time soon.

Predicting wildfire

Fire scientists use a variety of long and short-range imagery to determine vegetative cover, determine fuel type, and measure topography. Foresters from the NFS and BLM cruise federal lands, observing vegetation density, vegetation health, and vegetation hydration. Meteorologists track weather systems, especially during the hot, dry summer months and issue warnings of increased fire risk. Regions with heavy cover of dead or dry vegetation that also have steep topography are at particular risk for wildfire. If a fire starts near the bottom of steep terrain, it dries the vegetation above it before the fire reaches the vegetation, making it easier to ignite and burn. An enclosed shaft can act like a chimney, creating a draft of air and fanning flames to greater intensity.

Before and after photos of a Montana forest in the Bitterroot Valley in 1909

Bitterroot Valley fires of 1988

Dense stands of vegetation are more prone to fire. Forestry policy over the past 60 years has created very dense stands of timber and other vegetation. This is of special concern in the western US. Historically, tree density in much of the western US was between 10 and 50 trees per acre, depending upon local weather and climate conditions. Because fire prevention, logging, and grazing policies initiated in the 1950s prevented vegetation clearing, tree density in much of the West has risen to 200 to 1500 trees per acre. In dry climates such as the western US, densely packed trees remove more water from the soil, and that water is not replaced by precipitation. In the event of a drought, the trees are weakened even further, they are attacked by insects, and many die. Accumulations of weak and dead trees in close proximity to one another during subsequent dry periods make intense fires a certainty.

Preventing catastrophe

NFS foresters and other forestry scientists have begun advocating for the removal of more trees from federal lands by logging to reduce the burden of fuel. Others have advocated for increased grazing on some federal lands to reduce brush and dry grass. Clearly these proposals are not popular with conservation groups. Plans are being created that will allow fires to burn more naturally when they start so the overall accumulation of fuel will decline without igniting canopy fires that create so much damage.

Residents who live in or near wild lands are counseled, and in some cases, such as in San Diego County required, to create a "defensible perimeter" around their homes. A defensible perimeter is an area around the house in which:

- inflammable vegetation is cleared

- only low growing vegetation is planted near the house so fire cannot climb the vegetation to the roof

- fire resistant varieties of plants are used in landscaping

- tree branches are trimmed to prevent fire from climbing into the canopy

- "ladder fuels," dead vegetation leaning against or in close proximity to trees, are removed

- a fire break is created and maintained at least 30 feet away from the house.

Summary

Fire scientists use a variety of long- and short-range imagery and ground level observations to determine vegetative cover, determine fuel type, and measure topography. Meteorologists track weather systems, especially during the hot, dry summer months and issue warnings of increased fire risk. Because fire prevention, logging, and grazing policies initiated in the 1950's prevented vegetation clearing, tree density in much of the West has risen to 200 to 1500 trees per acre. In the event of a drought, the trees are weakened, attacked by insects, and many die. Accumulations of weak and dead trees in close proximity to one another during subsequent dry periods make intense fires a certainty. NFS foresters and other forestry scientists have begun advocating for increased logging and grazing on some federal lands to reduce fuel loads. These proposals are unpopular with conservation groups. Plans are being created that will allow fires to burn more naturally when they start so the overall accumulation of fuel will decline without igniting canopy fires that create so much damage. Residents who live in or near wild lands should create a "defensible perimeter" around their homes to reduce the likelihood of property loss.

Concept Reinforcement:

1. Why are fires in the western US increasing in severity, frequency, and duration?

2. How do scientists determine the risk of wildfire?

3. How can homeowners reduce their risk of property loss to wildfire?

Chapter 31 – Introduction to Health, Disease, and Astronomical Disasters

Chapter Objective:

- Introduce the various health, disease, and space disasters and investigate the science of these disasters

Introduction

In this section we will examine Epidemics, Pandemics, and Infectious Diseases, Famines, Solar Flares, and Impacts. Epidemics and Pandemics are large-scale outbreaks of diseases. Epidemics are localized to a specific geographic region and need not be infectious. Pandemics, on the other hand, are disease outbreaks that are global in scope and must be infectious diseases. Famines are localized, short-term periods of food scarcity. Famine can weaken populations to the point at which opportunistic diseases can cause illness and death. Solar flares are vast eruptions of plasma from the Sun's surface that occur as a result of the Sun's magnetic field lines becoming twisted by the Sun's rotation. Some magnetic lines become inverted and throw plasma from the Sun's atmosphere into space before crashing back to the surface. Impacts refer to large objects from space colliding with the Earth. The effect of an impact on the Earth is related to the size and composition of the body impacting the planet. Scientists speculate that an impact in the Gulf of Mexico just off the Yucatan peninsula was responsible for the extinction of the dinosaurs.

Crater Impact

Epidemics, pandemics, and infectious diseases

Epidemics, pandemics, and infectious diseases are studied by epidemiologists. Epidemiologists are medical doctors and scientists who study the patterns of an infectious disease outbreak, how the disease spreads in a population, factors that contribute to the spread of the disease, and ways to stop the spread of infectious disease. Epidemiologists use virology, bacteriology, mycology, parasitology, microbiology, pathology, anthropology, social science, political science, mathematics, and sophisticated computer modeling techniques to track the spread of a disease and how well efforts to contain the disease are working.

They must understand the kind of disease organism causing the epidemic, how the organism is transmitted, local customs that may make disease transmission easier, local customs that may prevent doctors from adequately treating the disease, and they must be able to predict where the disease will strike next so they can prevent it or catch the disease early in the population.

Famine

Famine is a short-term lack of sufficient food to sustain human life and activity in a geographically limited area. Note that famine is not a long-term phenomenon. Hunger, which is different, is a constant companion to millions of people all over the globe. But famine begins and ends, usually in conjunction with droughts, wars, or other disturbances. Famine usually elicits an emergency response from the community of nations. Nations with food surpluses attempt to send food and medical aid to the affected area. Unfortunately, in many cases, aid does not reach famine sufferers because of political revenge or corruption. Western nations are investigating new ways to deliver food aid that avoids these pitfalls.

Famine is the lack of sufficient food to sustain human life.

Solar flares

Solar flares are caused by massive magnetic eruptions on the surface of the Sun. Solar plasma, highly ionized, highly energetic particles, are blasted into space with tremendous energy. X-rays are deflected by the Earth's magnetosphere, but orbiting spacecraft and satellites can be damaged or destroyed by the highly charged particles that stream through the magnetosphere as a result of a solar flare. Astronauts in the path of a solar flare could be subjected to dangerous levels of radiation. Solar flares contribute to the aurora borealis and aurora australis near the Earth's poles.

Impacts refer to collision with the Earth of large-scale interplanetary bodies such as asteroids, meteors, and comets. Impacts of such a large magnitude would release tremendous forces as the object first penetrates the atmosphere and then strikes the planet. Enormous energy would be released as a result of such an impact. Water, soil, rocks, and organic debris would be ejected into the atmosphere to plummet to Earth hundreds, if not thousands of miles away. Enormous clouds of water vapor and dust would blanket the planet in darkness. Scientists speculate that the dinosaurs were wiped out by just such an impact off the Yucatan peninsula. There are several other large impact crater remnants on the planet indicating impacts have happened more than once. An exceptionally large impact with an object only somewhat smaller than Earth is hypothesized to have blasted enough material off the surface of our planet that the Moon formed from the debris. Clearly such an impact would destroy all life on Earth.

Summary

Epidemics and Pandemics are large-scale outbreaks of infectious diseases. Famines are localized, short-term periods of food scarcity. Solar flares are vast eruptions of plasma from the Sun's surface. Impacts refer to large objects from space colliding with the Earth.

Concept Reinforcement:

1. How are epidemics, pandemics, and infectious diseases related?

2. What is the difference between famine and hunger?

3. Why are scientists concerned about impacts?

Chapter 32 – Epidemics

- Introduce the various epidemics, and investigate the science of epidemics

Introduction

Epidemics and Pandemics are large-scale outbreaks of infectious diseases. Epidemics are localized to a specific geographic region. Pandemics, on the other hand, are disease outbreaks that are global in scope. In this section, we will become familiar with some of the epidemics that currently plague the world. Most, but not all of them are especially prevalent in the developing world. Children are especially susceptible to epidemic diseases because of their immature immune systems. Epidemiology is the science of epidemics. Epidemiologists study disease outbreaks and how disease spreads in a population.

Cholera

Cholera is caused by the bacterium Vibrio cholerae. Cholera infections are the result of eating contaminated food or drinking contaminated water. Cholera causes acute watery diarrhea and dehydration of the victim. Cholera can cause death by dehydration within 12 hours if it is not treated. Treatment includes rehydration therapy with electrolytes and antibiotic treatment. Cholera was one of the great killers of the pre-modern era. European and American armies typically lost more solders to cholera than in battle. Today, cholera is a frequent killer in Central and South America, Southeast Asia, India, and Africa. Most cholera victims are under the age of 5 or among the aged.

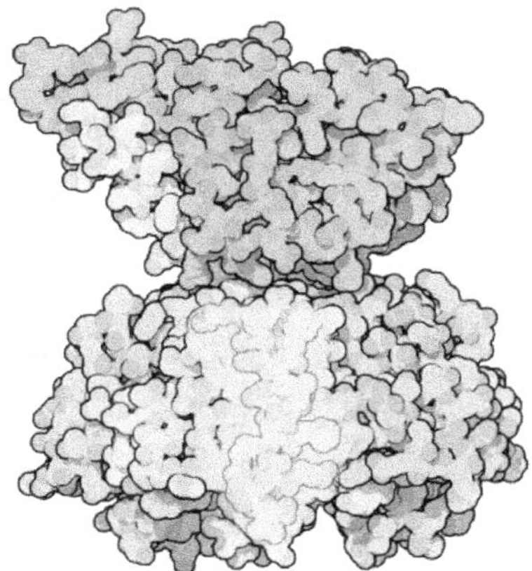

Illustration of the cholera toxin (in red)

Yellow fever is a viral disease that is transmitted by mosquitoes. Yellow fever is so called because of the jaundice that often results due to liver failure during the course of the disease. Yellow fever is one of several hemorrhagic fevers, which cause bleeding within the body. Yellow fever victims suffer from headaches, nausea, fever, and vomiting. Bleeding into the skin is also common. The disease may then go into a brief remission and the patient begins to feel better. The disease returns within a few days to cause massive internal bleeding, "coffee ground" vomit from bleeding into the digestive system, delirium, coma, and death. Yellow fever is preventable by vaccination. Mosquito eradication or suppression programs help control the spread of the disease. Yellow fever, combined with malaria, prevented the French from digging the Panama Canal. Only after mosquitoes were identified as the carriers of these two diseases and mosquito control efforts were initiated to quell the spread of the diseases could the United States complete the Canal.

Dengue Fever

Dengue fever, also known as break-bone fever because of the severe muscle and joint pain it causes, is a mosquito-borne viral disease that affects the tropics. Similar to Yellow Fever, Dengue fever is a hemorrhagic fever that causes death by internal bleeding. Fever, headache, and rash outbreaks are common initial signs of Dengue Fever. Platelet count, the particles in the blood responsible for clotting, falls. Small blood vessels beneath the skin on the chest and legs begin to rupture, forming petechiae. Victims may bleed internally, vomit blood, or bleed from the mucous membranes of the nose and mouth. Treatment includes rehydration therapy and in some cases platelet transfusion. There is no vaccine currently available. Mosquito control programs help reduce the incidence of the disease.

Malaria

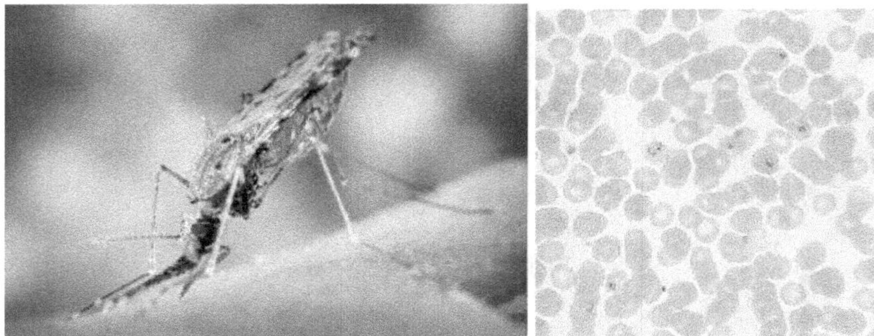

Malaria is spread by mosquitoes and causes a low red blood cell count to occur.

Malaria (Plasmodium spp.) is a protozoan blood parasite that is transmitted by mosquitoes. Malaria is endemic to central Africa and has spread to many tropical regions. Malaria affects over 515 million people and kills between 1 and 3 million people every year. The majority of deaths are children under the age of 5 in sub-Saharan Africa. In fact, malaria is probably the leading cause of death in children under 5 in Africa. Malaria causes anemia or low red blood cell count, fever, chills, shortness of breath, coma, and death. There is no vaccine for malaria. Malaria is treated with a variety of anti-malarial drugs including quinine and artemisinin, but resistant strains of malaria are appearing. Mosquito control programs are effective in slowing the spread of the disease.

The HumanImmunodeficiency Virus (HIV)is a retrovirus that uses RNAinstead of DNA as its genetic material. HIV attacks the CD4+ T lymphocytes, macrophages, and dendritic cells of the immune system. When the immune system can no longer function, the body becomes susceptible to many opportunistic diseases. The failure of the immune system that results from HIV infection is called Autoimmune Deficiency Syndrome, or AIDS. HIV is transmitted in blood, semen, vaginal fluids, and breast milk. HIVis spread by unprotected sex with infected individuals, needle sharing by illicit drug abusers, and from mother to infant at birth or by breastfeeding. There is currently no vaccine for HIV, although poten-tial vaccine candidates are being tested and screened. HIV treatment involves a complex regime of anti-retroviral drugs and support therapy. HIV/AIDS is especially acute in sub-Saharan Africa where 90 million adults are expected to be infected with the virus over the next few years. The spread of the disease in Africa is particularly distressing because it will leave behind an estimated 18 million orphans.

Summary

Cholera, Yellow Fever, Dengue Fever, Malaria, and HIV/AIDS are epidemic diseases that are responsible for the deaths of millions of people in the developing world every year. Many of these deaths are children under the age of 5. HIV/AIDS will leave millions of orphans in its wake and many of them will probably die of other diseases. Epidemiologists have studied each of these diseases and know how they are spread and how to slow or stop their spread. Howeverfinancial and social considerations in developing countries prevent epidemiologists from completing their work.

Concept Reinforcement:

1. What is the common disease vector for Yellow Fever, Dengue Fever, and Malaria and what can be done to slow their spread?

2. How are children disproportionately impacted by epidemic diseases?

3. Where are most epidemic and pandemic disease outbreaks found?

Chapter 33 – Understanding Epidemics

Chapter Objective:

- Explain how scientists measure, monitor and evaluate epidemics

Introduction

Epidemiologists are the medical scientists who study disease outbreaks, epidemics, and pandemics. They use techniques ranging from fieldwork including interviews of victims and their families, lab work, and complex computer modeling to measure, monitor, and evaluate the spread of disease. Because of the wide variety of diseases causing epidemics, from viruses in blood to obesity, epidemiologists must be broadly trained medical specialists. Epidemiologists follow a ten-step process to ensure success in tracking down a disease outbreak and stopping it.

Prepare for fieldwork

When a disease outbreak is reported, epidemiologists must research the disease to make certain they pack the correct tools and equipment to collect samples for the suspected disease. It is not a simple task to run back to the lab to pick up forgotten supplies when you are in a small village. Travel arrangements must be made, ground transportation must be arranged, visas and permissions must be granted, local officials must be identified and contacted, and the role the epidemiologists will play must be determined.

Establish the existence of an outbreak

Not all reports of disease outbreaks are true outbreaks. It is important to establish that a disease outbreak is truly occurring. Similar diseases may be misdiagnosed and reported together, reporting requirements may have changed, population size and distribution may have changed, and new medical personnel may be more vigilant in reporting diseases than their predecessors. Comparing records of disease occurrence from recent weeks, months, or the previous year may provide an accurate indication of true disease outbreak. In other cases, contacting local medical personnel may reveal an increase in disease prevalence.

Cases of a disease must be identified and enumerated. The clinical signs must be identified so people can be classified as having the disease. Where and when the disease occurs is critical information that should be collected at this time.

Describe and orient data

The cases observed, when, and where must be organized into a time and location tree to track the spread of the disease and attempt to locate its source. Epidemiologists can sometimes use the model developed by orienting the data to predict the expected length and number of people to be infected by the outbreak.

Develop hypotheses

When the data is described and oriented, hypotheses can be developed as to the likely source of the outbreak and how to stop it.

Evaluate hypotheses

Once hypotheses have been developed, epidemiologists can test them against observations in the field. Case studies can be carried out, and causative relationships established.

Refine hypotheses

In most cases, the initial hypotheses tested will contain some of the answers. In other cases they will be incorrect. In either case, once the hypotheses have been evaluated and weaknesses have been exposed, existing hypotheses can be refined or new ones proposed.

Implement control or prevention measures

Once the source of the outbreak and the means of transmission have been identified, measures to control or prevent the continued spread of the disease can be put in place.

When epidemiologists complete their work, they communicate their findings to local health authorities whose job is to develop and implement policy to prevent future outbreaks. Education of the public is frequently the best way to stop an outbreak. Many epidemic diseases are waterborne or mosquito-borne. Sanitizing water by boiling it and eradicating mosquito breeding grounds are ways local residents can dramatically reduce the probability of epidemic disease outbreaks.

Summary

Epidemiologists are the medical scientists who study disease outbreaks, epidemics, and pandemics. Epidemiologists follow a ten-step process to ensure success in tracking down a disease outbreak and stopping it.

The steps are:

- Prepare for field work

- Establish existence of an outbreak

- Define and identify cases

- Describe and orient data

- Develop hypotheses

- Evaluate hypotheses

- Refine hypotheses

- Implement control or prevention measures

- Communicate findings

Concept Reinforcement:

1. Why is preparation for fieldwork such an important step of the process of disease measurement, monitoring, and evaluation?

2. Not all outbreak reports are truly reports of outbreaks of diseases. Why?

3. What are two of the best ways to control or halt disease outbreaks?

Chapter 34 – Preventing Epidemics

Chapter Objective:

- Understand the role science plays in the prevention of an epidemic

Introduction

Epidemics, pandemics, and infectious diseases are studied by epidemiologists. Epidemiologists are medical doctors and scientists who study the patterns of an infectious disease outbreak, how the disease spreads in a population, factors that contribute to the spread of the disease, and ways to stop the spread of infectious disease. Epidemiologists use virology, bacteriology, mycology, parasitology, microbiology, pathology, nutrition, anthropology, social science, political science, mathematics, and sophisticated computer modeling techniques to track the spread of a disease and how well efforts to contain the disease are working. They must understand the kind of disease organism causing the epidemic, how the organism is transmitted, local customs that may make disease transmission easier, local customs that may prevent doctors from adequately treating the disease, and they must be able to predict where the disease will strike next so they can prevent it or catch the disease early in the population.

Virology, bacteriology, mycology, parasitology, microbiology, pathology, and nutrition

Diseases are caused by pathogenic viruses, bacteria, fungi, parasites and nutritional deficits. Many of these pathogenic organisms are microbes. Epidemiologists must understand the biology of the organisms they are hunting. Each organism has specific habitat requirements, transmission vectors, life cycles, and vulnerabilities. Each pathogen also has specific signs and symptoms that allow knowledgeable practitioners to properly identify and treat victims. The sciences of virology, bacteriology, mycology, parasitology, microbiology, and pathology provide insight into the lives, needs, and weaknesses of each organism as well as its signs and symptoms. Epidemiologists use this knowledge to track down disease reservoirs, limit the spread of the disease, and recommend treatment options.

Nutrition can cause disease outbreaks in populations in specific geographic regions. For example, soils in the upper Midwestern US are deficient in iodine, and crops grown there do not provide sufficient dietary iodine to local residents. This discovery by epidemiologists and nutritionists lead to the introduction of iodized salt in the US to eliminate the prevalence of goiter, an iodine deficiency disease. The recent obesity epidemic in the US is another example of a nutritional disorder that has broad effects.

Anthropology, social science, and political science

Once epidemiologists have determined what disease is causing an outbreak, they propose measures to prevent the spread of the disease or eliminate it. However, many cultures do not permit certain measures to be used. Other cultural and political difficulties can be encountered when epidemiologists attempt to communicate their findings and recommendations. For example, in many African nations, sexual practices and women's status are such that the disease is likely to continue to spread regardless of the knowledge of the cause of HIV/AIDS. For a woman to request her husband use a condom in many cultures is equivalent to a statement that she intends to be unfaithful to him. Women do not have the right to demand sexual partners use condoms. Government authorities have gone so far as to claim that AIDS is not caused by HIV and is an American plot to control the country. Some governments refuse to admit the existence of a problem for fear of appearing weak. Other governments do not permit discussion of sexual matters for socio-religious reasons.

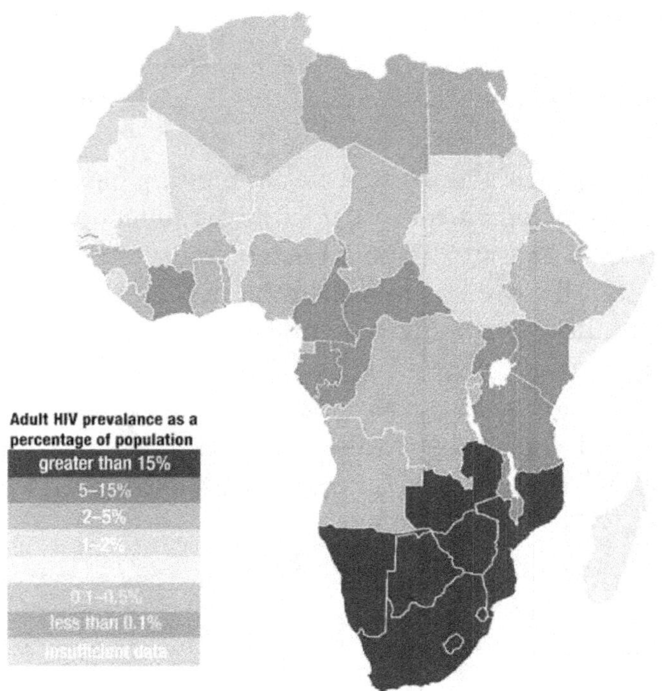

Adult HIV prevalence in Africa

Epidemiologists must be aware of these limitations and develop methods to protect the populace from disease despite these barriers. One effective technique in some parts of sub-Saharan Africa is for health workers to travel to villages and sing songs about condoms and condom use to prevent HIV/AIDS. Songs are the cultural method of information transmission and historical memory in the region, and the songs are passed from village to village

Epidemiologists use mathematical models and statistical analyses to model the progression of a disease and the effects of control measures. Epidemiologists conduct experiments and collect data which must be analyzed statistically. Information regarding where an outbreak is occurring, the timeframe of the outbreak, the progress of the outbreak, and measures being used to slow its progress, is analyzed to monitor and evaluate a disease outbreak. Computer programming skills are required to work with such complex models.

Summary

Epidemiologists are medical doctors and scientists who study the patterns of an infectious disease outbreak. They use biological, social, mathematical, and computer sciences to study disease outbreaks and the effects of preventive measures on the progress of the outbreak. Disease control and prevention measures must take the biology of the disease as well as the social and political implications of the disease into account to be successful.

Concept Reinforcement:

1. Why is knowledge of the biology of disease organisms and diseases important to epidemiologists?

2. Why are anthropological, social, and political sciences important to epidemiologists?

3. How are mathematics and computer science important to epidemiologists?

Chapter 35 – Predicting Epidemics

Chapter Objective:

- Analyze how we can use science to predict epidemics, and prevent catastrophe

Introduction

The enormous cost of epidemics and pandemics, both in terms of economic losses and loss of lives, has driven public health officials to prepare for possible disease outbreaks. Health officials at the US Centers for Disease Control and Prevention (CDC) have used the flu pandemic of 1918 as a model to develop methods of predicting potential epidemics and how communities should respond. The result is a nine-step checklist for health authorities to use in the event of an epidemic.

Community preparedness leadership and networking

The first step in any response to a potential epidemic is to identify who will be responsible for ensuring the necessary steps are taken to prevent the spread of the outbreak. Local leaders must have plans in place delineating responsibilities, jurisdictional and cross-jursidictional responsibilities, communications, and command and control facilities. Emergency response drills must be planned, conducted, and evaluated.

Disease surveillance

Medical personnel are required to report certain communicable diseases to national health authorities. Once a disease that has the potential to cause an epidemic is identified in an area, medical personnel are notified and disease surveillance is increased. Communication between human and animal health care practitioners must be fostered as many epidemic diseases also affect animals.

Public health and clinical laboratories

Clinical diagnostic laboratories should have disease surveillance plans in place to detect reportable diseases and the initial stages of an outbreak. They must have plans in place to handle a surge in demand in the event of an epidemic. They must provide health care workers with instructions for safe sample collection methods and instructions for proper sample collection. Damaged samples are not useful in the event of an outbreak.

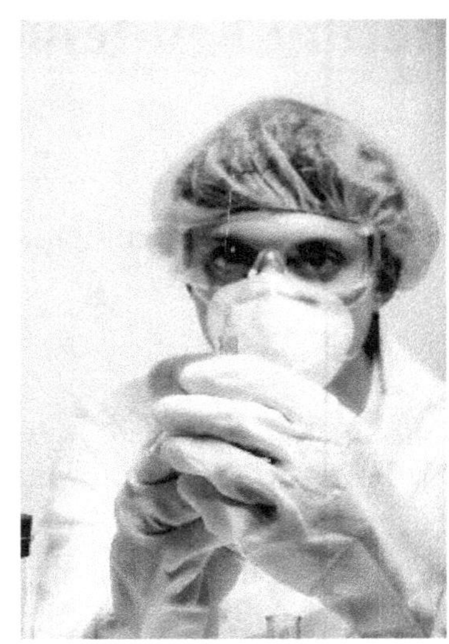

Healthcare workers are the front-line combatants in the event of an epidemic. They must know how to keep themselves safe so they may continue to function. They must be prepared for the surge in demand and the strains it can place on families and healthcare workers. They must remain aware of the needs of patients other than those who are epidemic victims. Plans to handle increased numbers of bodies in the morgue must be written. All plans must be tested from time to time in emergency preparedness drills.

Communications to healthcare workers are critical during an epidemic. Communications systems must be in place before the emergency happens. Contact information for current and former healthcare workers must be accurate and accessible.

Procurement, storage, distribution, and monitoring of vaccines must be a priority in the event of an epidemic. Vaccine recipients must be prioritized. Vaccine stocks must be kept secure against theft or destruction due to public unrest in an epidemic. Local residents must receive information explaining when and where they will receive vaccinations. Plans must be tested periodically to ensure they are effective.

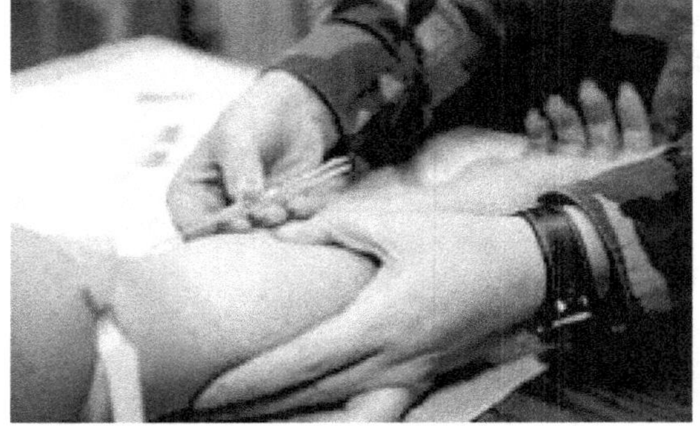

Vaccines are a priority in the event of an epidemic.

Antiviral drug distribution and use

As for vaccines, plans must be developed for the procurement, storage, distribution, and monitoring of antiviral drugs, prioritization of recipients, security of stockpiles, and promulgation of information to residents. Plans must be tested periodically to ensure they are effective.

Community disease control and prevention (including managing travel-related risk of disease transmission)

Restriction of movement, formerly known as quarantine, is a key element of slowing the spread of infectious diseases. School closings are especially effective as children are frequently the most likely human vectors of disease. Cancellation of public transportation services and large public events eliminates the potential for large numbers of healthy people to be exposed to contagious individuals. Residents can be informed about the need to restrict their movement and asked to cooperate.

Public health communications

The best method of combating epidemics is preventing their occurrence in the first place. Public health awareness campaigns coordinated among public health officials, non-profit organizations such as the Red Cross, and educators can do more to prevent disease than almost any other measure, and at a low cost. Health entities should communicate among themselves to ensure that a consistent, research-based message is distributed to residents.

Workforce support: psychosocial considerations and information needs

Healthcare workers work long hours during an epidemic and meet the needs of many more patients than they would normally see. The long hours, lack of communication with and knowledge of their families, suffering, and high death toll can reduce the psychological ability of healthcare workers to function. Behavioral specialists can develop means of helping healthcare workers remain as functional as possible and to recover after the trauma of seeing so much suffering and death.

Summary

The enormous cost, both in terms of economic losses and loss of lives, of epidemics and pandemics has driven public health officials to prepare for possible disease outbreaks. They have created a nine-step checklist for health authorities to use in the event of an epidemic, including:

- community preparedness leadership and networking

- disease surveillance

- public health and clinical laboratories

- healthcare and public health partners

- infection control and clinical guidelines

- vaccine distribution and use

- antiviral drug distribution and use

- community disease control and prevention

- public health communications

- workforce support.

Concept Reinforcement:

1. What role should community leaders play in the event of an epidemic?

2. What are the concerns that must be addressed regarding vaccines during an epidemic?

3. Why is psychological support for healthcare workers so important during an epidemic?

Chapter 36 – Epidemics and Pandemics

Chapter Objective:

- Compare and contrast epidemics and pandemics

Introduction

Epidemics and Pandemics are large-scale outbreaks of diseases. Epidemics are localized to a specific geographic region and need not be infective. Pandemics, on the other hand, are disease outbreaks that are global in scope and must be infectious diseases. In this section, we will compare and contrast epidemics and pandemics using examples to clarify the difference.

Influenza

Every year, hundreds of thousands of people are hospitalized, and tens of thousands are killed in the US by one strain or another of the influenza virus, the flu. The flu is spread from animals to humans, with swine and chickens being major reservoirs of the disease. Approximately once or twice every twenty years, a flu pandemic occurs. The reasons are not yet understood, but a particularly virulent strain of the disease develops and spreads rapidly throughout the population killing hundreds of thousands of people and sickening millions. The Flu pandemic of 1918 was the worst pandemic on record, with over 25 million deaths worldwide and 500,000 in the US. More people died as a result of the flu than all of the casualties of World War I combined.

Black Plague

Illustration of the Black Plague

In the mid-14th century CE,the bubonic plague ravaged the populations of China,North-ern Africa, and Europe. Some epidemiologists classify the Plague as a series of epidemics, small-scale outbreaks in local populations without wider effects. Otherspoint to the slow rate of travel in the 14th century and argue that the plague was carried around the world by merchants and travelers very rapidly for the time period, classifying the Plague as a pan-demic. There is also some discussion about the disease organism that caused the outbreaks in each location. If different bacteria caused the outbreaks, they would be categorized as epidemics. If the same species of bacterium caused the outbreaks, the pandemic argument would be strengthened. The Black Plague is estimated to have killed nearly a quarter of the world's population, and between one and two thirds of Europe's population.

Ebola

Ebola is one of several viral diseases that cause hemorrhagic fevers. Ebola epidemics are usually widely publicized because of the highly dramatic nature of death. The Ebola vi-ruses are so deadly that between 50 and 90% of Ebola victims die. The disease usually kills its victims within 5 to 7 days, and incapacitates them much more rapidly. Because Ebola kills so quickly and typically occurs in such remote regions, it is unlikely that Ebola will ever become a pandemic widespread threat to human health.

Severe acute respiratory syndrome (SARS)

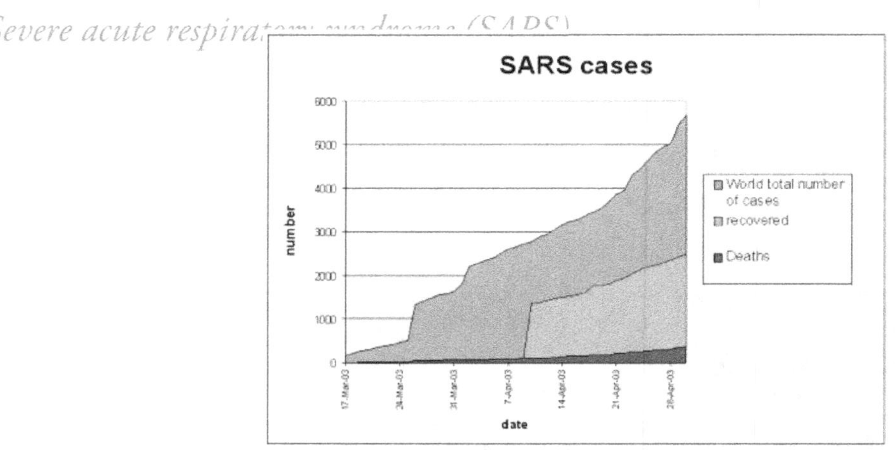

Cases of SARS

Severe Acute Respiratory Syndrome (SARS) first appeared in Chinain 2002. SARS rap-idly spread by airborne transmission, and traveled quickly around the world as a resul of airline travel. SARS never reached pandemic proportions, as most international cases could be traced to people were either from the affected area or had recently traveled t the area. However,it had the potential to do so, and had global authorities not been a vigilant as they were or responded more slowly than they had it almost certainly woul have be-come the first new disease of the 20th century to become a pandemic.

Obesity

Obesity is defined as a body mass index (BMI) of over 30 kg/m2. Overweight individuals have a BMI of 25 – 29.9. The US has the highest rates of obesity in the world. Approximately 1 in 8 children, and 1 in 3 adults is obese in America. Nearly two thirds of the adult population in the US is overweight or obese. Obesity contributes to heart disease, stroke, cancer, sleep apnea, and diabetes. The cost of obesity and overweight in the US is estimated at nearly $100 billion in direct medical costs and lost productivity. Direct medical costs account for approximately 75% of that cost. As a result of the increase in obese and overweight Americans, diabetes has risen to rank as the 7th leading cause of death in the US. However, obesity is not an infectious disease, so although the consequences of the obesity epidemic are severe and widespread, it is not classified as a pandemic.

Summary

Epidemics and Pandemics are large-scale outbreaks of diseases. Epidemics are localized to a specific geographic region and need not be infective. Pandemics, on the other hand, are outbreaks of infectious diseases that are global in scope. Obesity, Ebola, and SARS are examples of epidemics. In most years, influenza is no more than an epidemic either. However, once or twice every 20 years influenza outbreaks achieve pandemic proportions, killing hundreds of thousands in the US alone. The Black Plague could arguably be placed in either category. Future investigations into the causes of the Black Plague across such a large regional and time frame may answer the question of how many disease organisms were responsible for one of the most disastrous disease outbreaks in human history.

Concept Reinforcement:

1. Why might the Black Plague have been an epidemic? A pandemic?

2. Why is Ebola unlikely to ever become a pandemic?

3. Why is obesity an epidemic and not a pandemic, even though it is so widespread?

Chapter 37 – Understanding Famines

Chapter Objective:

- Explain how scientists measure, monitor and evaluate famines

Introduction

In order to discuss famine, it must first be clearly defined as there tends to be much confusion about the meaning of the term. Famine is one type of Hunger. Hunger is defined as the long-term lack of sufficient food for a person to carry out the normal activities of daily life, the pain associated with lack of sufficient food, and the persistent desire for food. Hunger is divided into several categories. Under-nutrition is the state of not receiving enough nu-trients to carry out the basic processes of life. Malnutrition is the overabundance or under-abundance of one or more nutrients in a diet that may otherwise be adequate. Famine is a short-term geographically localized lack of sufficient food to feed a population.

The primary cause of famine in the world today is war. Refugees' crops are left behind or taken from them, and food aid is in short supply or cannot pass through combat lines to reach the hungry. Other causes of famine include drought, seasonal famine in which harvested crops do not provide enough food to last until the next harvest, natural disasters, and poverty. Occasionally, political office holders will withhold food as a weapon against the political supporters of opposition parties.

Hunger in general, and famine in particular, disproportionately affects children. Estimates of as many as 1 out of every 5 childhood deaths of children under the age of 5 are either directly or indirectly a result of hunger. During famine, the victims are even more disproportionately children.

Measuring, monitoring and evaluating famines

Scientists measure rainfall, market prices of grains, livestock conditions, rangeland status, and changes in livelihood profiles to determine the onset of and measure the severity of a famine. Changes in these indicators are monitored during the famine to predict the duration and severity of the famine so relief efforts can be scaled up to meet the needs of the affected population.

The ability of a population to produce its own food from fully capable to fully dependent upon outside aid are monitored and used to evaluate the severity of a famine. As a famine progresses, farmers typically cannot keep up with demand to feed even their own families. Increases in food prices affect the ability of people, especially the very poor, to purchase food and other necessary items. Much of the developing world earns no more than $1 per day. Clearly such poor people cannot withstand many economic shocks before becoming unable to purchase food. Eventually, the local economy slows and grinds to a halt.

Weather forecasts are incorporated into the monitoring of the famine. Droughts and flooding both cause famine and are dependent upon the weather. Weather forecasters use climate models, radar imagery, and satellite imagery to predict weather conditions that contribute to famine. It can then be determined whether or not the conditions will abate in time for crops to be planted or recover.

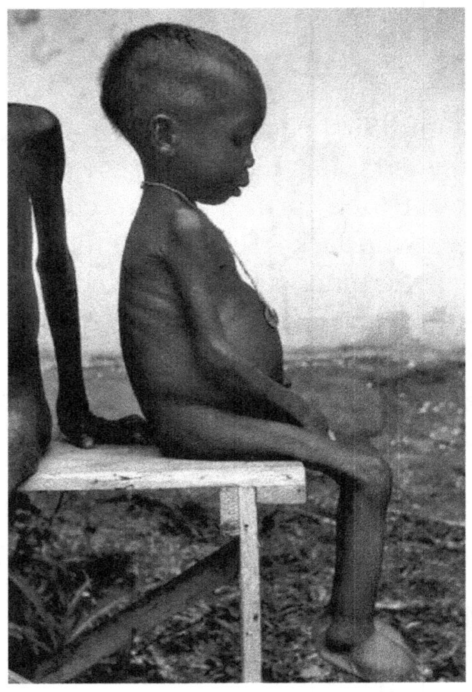

Symptoms of kwashiorkor, a nutritional disease caused by protein insufficiency, include swollen bellies and muscle wasting.

Nutritional benchmarks are utilized to measure, monitor, and evaluate the effect of the famine on the population's health. Wasting, or weight loss, due to famine, the presence and prevalence of nutritional diseases such as kwashiorkor, overall death rate, and death rate for children under the age of 5 are measured to monitor the famine and evaluate its severity.

The USAID and other international food and relief agencies use the following scales to monitor and evaluate famine.

Level	Phrase	Lives	Livelihood
0	Food secure	Crude Mortality Rate (CMR) < 0.2/10,000/day and/or Wasting < 2.3%	Cohesive social system; food prices stable; Coping strategies not utilized
1	Food insecure	0.2 <= CMR <0.5/10,000/day and/or 2.3% <= Wasting < 10%	Cohesive social system; Food prices unstable; Seasonal shortages; Reversible coping strategies taken
2	Food crisis	0.5 <= CMR < 1/10,000/day, 10% <= Wasting < 20%, and/or prevalence of edema	Social system stressed but largely cohesive; Dramatic rise in food and basic items prices; Adaptive mechanisms begin to fail; Increase in irreversible coping strategies
3	Famine	1 <= CMR < 5/10,000/day, 20% <= Wasting < 40%, and/or prevalence of edema	Clear signs of social breakdown; markets begin to collapse; coping strategies exhausted and survival strategies (migration in search of help, abandonment of weaker members of the community) adopted; affected population identifies food scarcity as the major societal problem
4	Severe famine	5 <= CMR <15/10,000/day, Wasting >= 40%, and/or prevalence of edema	Widespread social breakdown; markets close; survival strategies widespread; affected population identifies food scarcity as the major societal problem
5	Extreme famine	CMR >= 15/10,000/day	Complete social breakdown; widespread mortality; affected population identifies food scarcity as the major societal problem

Category	Phrase	Mortality range
A	Minor famine	0-999
B	Moderate famine	1,000-9,999
C	Major famine	10,000-99,999
D	Great famine	100,000-999,999
E	Catastrophic famine	1,000,000 and over

Summary

Famine is a short-term geographically localized lack of sufficient food to feed a population. The primary cause of famine in the world today is war. Other causes of famine include drought, seasonal famine, natural disasters, and poverty. Occasionally, political office holders will withhold food as a weapon against the political supporters of opposition parties. Scientists measure rainfall, market prices of grains, livestock conditions, rangeland status, and changes in livelihood profiles to determine the onset of and measure the severity of a famine.

Concept Reinforcement:

1. Compare and contrast Hunger and Famine.

2. What factors do scientists monitor to measure, monitor, and evaluate famine?

3. Why do even minor increases in food prices, especially grains, cause such major increases in the potential for famine?

Chapter 38 – Preventing Famines

Chapter Objective:

- Understand the role science plays in the prevention of famines

Introduction

With the exception of war and civil strife, famine has its roots in the environment and the ability of an environment to support a population. The soil, surface water, and precipitation in a region must be sufficient to meet the needs of the crops being grown. The UN Food and Agriculture Organization states that "…little progress has been made in preventing the causes of famine–the number of major disasters increased four-fold between the 1960s and 1980s…" Drought and land degradation continue to contribute to famine, and in fact have resulted in increased numbers of cases of famine during the same time period.

Soil

Examples of desertification

Soil losses in the developing world are extremely high. Poor cropping practices coupled with drought or torrential rains blow or wash away topsoil at an alarming rate. Trees are cut down for firewood for cooking and soil losses escalate. Soil degradation reduces the fertility of the remaining soil and reduces the ability of the soil to retain water in drought-prone regions. Soil nutrient levels are of particular concern because plants absorb key micromineral nutrients from the soil. The micronutrients are transferred to humans when people consume the plants. Degradation of the soil not only lowers crop output, but also degrades the nutrient quality of the crop it produces.

Precipitation

Crops and livestock in most of the developing world are extremely dependent upon precipitation for their water needs. In areas where rainfall amounts are often limited, crops do not receive enough water to survive. They wither, turn brown, and die. Grasses do not grow, depriving livestock of feed. Grazing animals are forced to consume every bit of plant material they can find, and the resultant overgrazing in arid regions speeds the process of desertification. In Niger, nearly 620,000 acres, almost 970 square miles, are lost each year to desertification because of poor agricultural practices. In parts of the world where seasonal monsoons bring torrential downpours lasting for days, water can drown crops in the fields, carry livestock away in floods, and ruin stored seed grains and harvested crops.

Surface water

In drought-prone regions, surface water can be used to irrigate crops and provide drinking water for livestock. But in drought years, surface waters may prove insufficient for both purposes. Surface water can also become contaminated with heavy metals from industrial and mining operations nearby because of lax environmental regulations. As droughts continue and water levels shrink, contaminants become more and more concentrated. Livestock drinking from contaminated water may die, and crops may concentrate toxins to the point that the crop becomes toxic as well.

Research reduces food insecurity

Because science has clearly documented the need for water resource development and soil conservation practices, international aid agencies and non-governmental organizations (NGOs) have begun to focus on improved agricultural practices. Improved irrigation procedures have been implemented, foot treadle water pumps have been installed, and water collection systems have been put in place to store water in drought-prone regions. Soil conservation measures are being implemented to reclaim desert land for crops and livestock grazing.

Irrigation system in Turkey

Plant scientists and agronomists have developed drought-resistant varieties of crops. Other new crops can improve soil fertility even while producing a useful crop for farmers to eat. NGOs and governmental aid agencies are making these new varieties available to farmers in drought-prone regions. Livestock production systems that focus on smaller species with lower feed requirements are being introduced to farmers in developing countries. Rabbits and poultry do not need as much space and are easier to care for in the event of a drought or flood.

Trees are being replanted to restore the availability of edible fruits and nuts as well as to hold the soil in place. Solar stoves are being introduced to reduce the need for firewood and eliminate the often long-trek for women who must forage for firewood.

Summary

Famine's roots are inextricably intertwined with the environment. Poor agricultural techniques, burgeoning populations, and poverty create the conditions for famine even in areas not suffering from civil or political strife. Scientific research has demonstrated the need for better soil and water conservation efforts, and created the methods to conserve both soil and water. Scientists have developed improved crop varieties and livestock production systems that improve the soil while feeding the population. Improved cooking methods reduce the need for wood and prevent further losses of trees.

Concept Reinforcement:

1. What are the causes of famine other than civil strife and war?

2. What are the effects of soil degradation on crops and crop production?

3. Why are farmers in developing countries encouraged to produce rabbits and poultry instead of goats, sheep, or cows?

Chapter 39 – Predicting Famines

* Analyze how we can use science to predict famines, and prevent catastrophe

Introduction

Predicting famine is difficult. Many famine prone locales are in the midst of civil war, social unrest, or are governed by repressive regimes that do not want outside agencies entering their country unescorted. However, these factors are indicators of the likelihood of famine.

Predicting famine

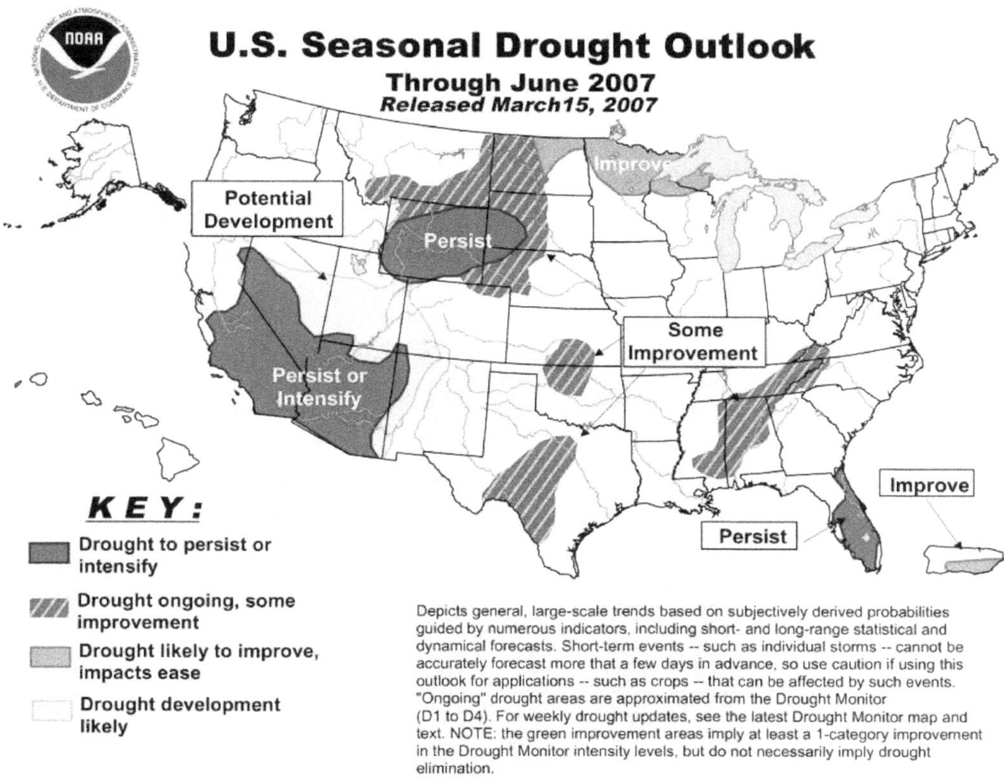

Scientists can use satellite imagery to estimate the potential for poor harvests or crop failures in areas they cannot enter. The National Oceanic and Atmospheric Administration (NOAA) operates a number of satellites in geosynchronous orbits that can determine the vigor and density of vegetation on the surface, rainfall estimation, and the location of the Intertropical Convergence Zone (ITCZ). Images from near red, infrared, and microwave, imaging systems on NOAA weather satellites and telecommunications satellites are processed by NASA and the US Geological Survey (USGS). The ITCZ is an area where the Trade Winds from both hemispheres converge, essentially cancelling one another out. The air in the region is heated by the Sun and rises vertically, creating intense precipitation. The

ITCZ wanders from the equator to the north or south as the seasons change, and it moves further when over land than over water because of uneven heating. From the satellite data, scientists generate a water requirements satisfaction index that informs them how well the amount of rainfall has satisfied the needs of the crops grown in a locale.

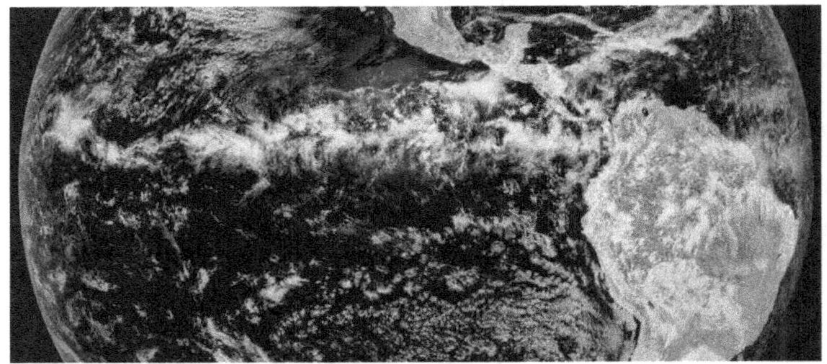

The ITCZ is the band of bright white clouds that cuts across the center of the image.

Scientists also create livelihood profiles to predict how well people in a given region are able to meet their needs for food, water, and shelter. They assess the hazards to which a region is vulnerable and combine this data into a series of spreadsheets that can predict economic risks to the population's livelihood.

When the weather and livelihood data are combined, scientists can predict whether crops in an area are receiving enough water, are likely to receive enough water, their state of health, and the ability of a region to withstand economic adversity. From this estimate, they can predict the probability of famine in the region.

Famine scene

Preventing catastrophe

The Famine Early Warning System Network (FEWSNET) operated by the US Agency for International Development (USAID) has created a seven-step process for responding to famine to reduce the impact of famine on the population.

Coordination and preparation of the response planning process. Plans must be prepared and put in place that designate who will do what, and when and how they will do it.

Needs assessment. When a famine or other food emergency strikes, the needs of those affected must be determined so an appropriate response can be planned to alleviate their suffering.

Develop response plans. Contingency plans should be drafted that address ways to respond to food emergencies based on historic famine needs and predicted needs based on the data used to predict famine in the region. The contingency plans can be adapted as needed into a Response Plan based on the results of the needs assessment phase.

Plan implementation. The Response Plan is immediately put into action.

Monitoring and evaluation of response, impact and changes in needs. The results of the Response Plan must be monitored and evaluated continuously to ensure appropriate aid is reaching famine victims and their suffering is being alleviated.

Adjust Response Plan. In the event monitoring and evaluation illuminate shortcomings of the Response Plan it can be modified to address its shortcomings.

Phase out. Once the emergency is over, local residents will need assistance returning their lives to normal. They may not have seeds available for next year's crop as the seeds may have been eaten. They may need relocation assistance as many victims will have moved to aid stations and must now return to their homes. Famine can create a number of medical problems from both the weakening of the victims' bodies and the overcrowding and unsanitary conditions that frequently exist in and around refugee camps.

During and immediately following the Phase out period, an in-depth evaluation of the response should be undertaken. Successes should be highlighted as well as failures. A detailed list of lessons learned should be created and integrated into planning for the next food emergency.

Summary

Scientists consider local political climates, civil war and unrest, and estimates of crop production in each year to predict the possibility of famine in a region. They use ground observations where and when they can, but must often rely on satellite data to form their estimates. Contingency plans are made in the event a famine is predicted and a seven-step process including:

- Coordination and preparation of the response planning process

- Needs assessment

- Develop response plans

- Plan implementation

- Monitoring and evaluation of response, impact and changes in needs

- Adjust Response Plan

- Phase out is followed to ensure success. A post-operational evaluation is conducted and lessons learned are incorporated into future planning.

Concept Reinforcement:

1. Why is it so difficult to obtain data to predict the possibility of famine?

2. What kind of satellite imagery is used to predict famine and how is it processed?

3. What are the 7 steps used to prevent catastrophe during a famine?

Chapter 40 – Understanding Solar Flares

- Explain how scientists measure, monitor and evaluate solar flares

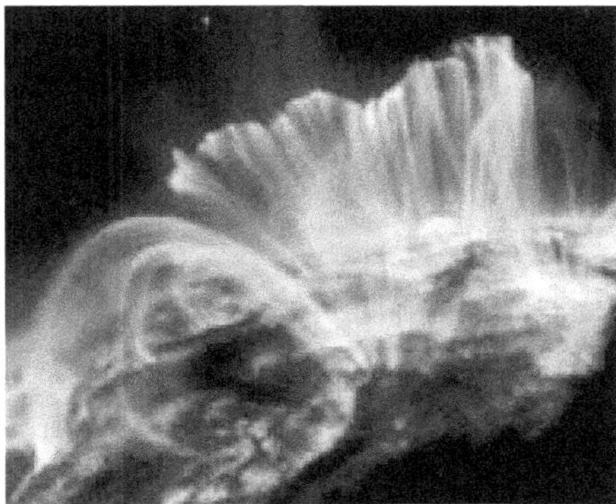

Solar Flare

Introduction

Solar flares are vast eruptions of plasma from the Sun's surface that occur as a result of the Sun's magnetic field lines becoming twisted by the Sun's rotation. Some magnetic lines become inverted and throw plasma from the Sun's atmosphere into space before crashing back to the surface. Solar plasma, highly ionized, highly energetic particles, are blasted into space with tremendous energy. X-rays are deflected by the Earth's magnetosphere, but orbiting spacecraft and satellites can be damaged or destroyed by the highly charged particles that stream through the magnetosphere as a result of a solar flare. Astronauts in the path of a solar flare could be subjected to dangerous levels of radiation. Solar flares contribute to the aurora borealis and aurora australis near the Earth's poles.

Measuring, monitoring and evaluating solar flares

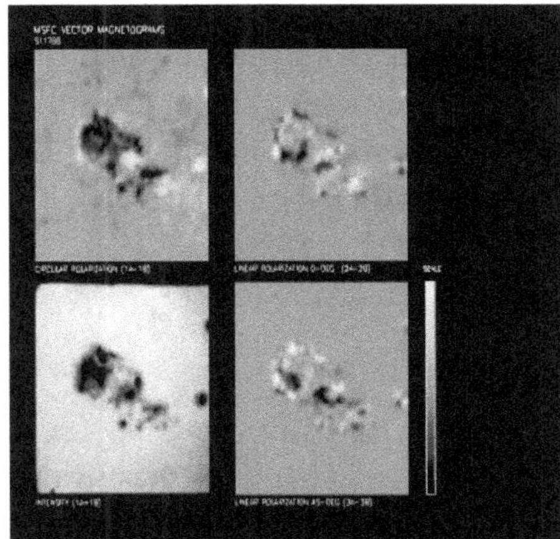

Vector magnetograph of an active region on the surface of the Sun.

Solar flares are a result of the magnetic activity of the Sun, and can be measured using a magnetograph. The Marshall Space Flight Center Vector Magnetograph Facility in Huntsville, AL, conducts vector magnetic field measurements of the Sun. Magnetographs measure the polarization of light from the Sun. Circular polarization of light indicates the strength of the magnetic field in line with the viewer (forward and backward). Linear polarization of light indicates the strength and direction of the magnetic field perpendicular to the viewer (side to side).

Marshall Space Flight Center Vector Magnetograph (white) and H-α telescope (gold).

Solar flares can be seen in the visible light spectrum, and are best viewed using the light emitted by hydrogen atoms in the red region of the solar spectrum. Most observatories that investigate solar flares have an H-α filter that allows them to see only the red light emitted by hydrogen to clearly identify and envision the flare. A few observatories like the Marshall Space Flight Center Vector Magnetograph Facility have combined both instruments into one so the visual image and the magnetic field lines can be overlaid easily.

Geostationary Operational Environmental Satellites (GOES) operated by the National Weather Service (NWS) are capable of detecting and recording the soft X-ray emissions resulting from solar flares. The Hinode satellite launched by Japan observes the Sun in the visible, extreme ultraviolet (UV), and X-ray bands as well as its magnetic fields. NASA's Solar and Heliospheric Observatory (SOHO) satellite observes X-ray emissions from solar flares.

X-rays and UV radiation from solar flares can cause disruption in radio transmissions, and satellites can be damaged by ionized particles. The disruption and damage can be measured and used as an indirect measure of the strength of the flare. Solar flare activity is monitored to help satellite operators avoid damage to their spacecraft.

Summary

Solar flares are vast eruptions of plasma from the Sun's surface that occur as a result of the Sun's magnetic field lines becoming twisted by the Sun's rotation. Solar flares are best observed using the light emitted by hydrogen atoms in the red region of the solar spectrum. However, extreme UV and soft X-ray observations are also excellent sources of information about flares. Vector magnetic field measurements of solar flares provide information about the strength and direction of the magnetic fields that generated the flares.

Concept Reinforcement:

1. What is a solar flare?

2. What is the best visible light spectrum for observing solar flares?

3. In addition to magnetographs and H-α filtered visible light telescopes, how else can solar flares be observed?

Chapter 41 – The Science of Solar Flares

- Understand the role science plays in solar flares

Introduction

Solar flares are vast eruptions of plasma from the Sun's surface that occur as a result of the Sun's magnetic field lines becoming twisted by the Sun's rotation. Some magnetic lines become inverted and throw plasma from the Sun's atmosphere into space before crashing back to the surface. Solar plasma, highly ionized, highly energetic particles, are blasted into space with tremendous energy. X-rays are deflected by the Earth's magnetosphere, but orbiting spacecraft and satellites can be damaged or destroyed by the highly charged particles that stream through the magnetosphere as a result of a solar flare. Astronauts in the path of a solar flare could be subjected to dangerous levels of radiation. Solar flares contribute to the aurora borealis and aurora australis near the Earth's poles.

The of science in solar flares

The Sun's magnetic field is probably the source of most, if not all, of the Sun's activity. Sunspots, solar flares, puffs, and solar mass ejections all result from changes in the Sun's magnetic field. The Sun's magnetic field is generated by the movement of ions in the solar plasma. As the ions flow, they create an electric current. An electrical current generates a magnetic field around it. The Sun's magnetic fields are capable of trapping hot, ionized gasses within the magnetic field lines.

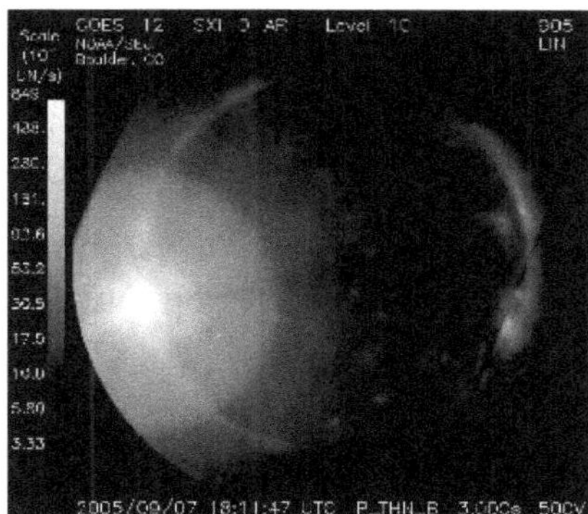

Image of a solar flare

The Sun's magnetic field progresses through solar maxima and minima, gradually strength-ening and weakening over a 22-year period. Scientists do not yet understand why. We see sunspot cycles and the incidence of solar flares increase and decrease over an 11-year cycle in the same fashion as a result of the changes in the Sun's magnetic field. The solar maxima and minima have profound effects on Earth. Periods of cold that last for several years have been observed to coincide with solar minima, and warmer periods have likewise coincided with solar maxima.

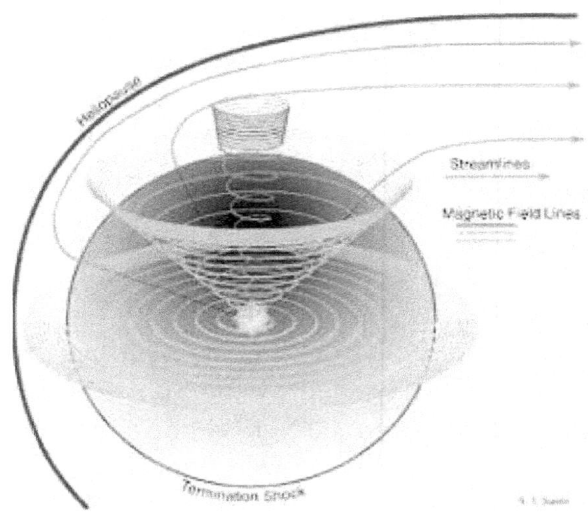

The coiled magnetic field lines of the Sun.

Because the Sun spins rapidly, but the magnetic field lines radiate outwardly perpendicular to the surface, the field lines are twisted, much like a garden hose when it is rolled up. Sometimes the lines cross and become broken. When this happens, the plasma and gasses trapped within the field lines can be ejected from the surface of the Sun with incredible force in a solar flare. Solar flares involve rapid heating of the solar corona, chromosphere and sometimes photosphere, to temperatures as high as 20,000,000 degrees F. Solar flares create emission of energetic photons and particles, and ejection of mass and magnetic fields from the Sun. The energy released is equivalent to over 1 million hydrogen bombs. There is some debate within the scientific community whether solar mass ejections and solar flares are the same phenomenon or different.

The solar ejecta speeds through space to wreak havoc on orbiting satellites and poses grave danger to astronauts. It creates intense auroras at the Earth's poles, can interrupt radio transmissions, sometimes for days, and can severely disrupt or damage power grids.

Scientists measure the X-rays, ultraviolet rays, and ionized particles released in solar flares to devise methods of protecting delicate orbiting instruments and astronauts. They also investigate methods of shielding Earthbound infrastructure such as power grids and radio communications systems. Climate models must account for solar maxima and minima to accurately predict climate change and its effects.

Summary

Solar flares are vast eruptions of plasma from the Sun's surface that occur as a result of the Sun's magnetic field lines becoming twisted by the Sun's rotation. Solar flares involve rapid heating of the solar corona, chromosphere and sometimes photosphere, to temperatures as high as 20,000,000 degrees F. Solar ejecta speeds through space to wreak havoc on orbiting satellites, poses grave danger to astronauts, creates intense auroras at the Earth's poles, can interrupt radio transmissions, and can severely disrupt or damage power grids. Scientists devise methods of protecting delicate orbiting instruments and astronauts, Earthbound infrastructure such as power grids and radio communications systems, and develop accurate climate models by studying solar flares and the Sun's magnetic field that create them.

Concept Reinforcement:

1. How does the Sun's magnetic field create a solar flare?

2. How does the Sun create its magnetic field?

3. Why do scientists study solar flares?

Chapter 42 – Predicting Solar Flares

- Analyze how we can use science to predict solar flares, and prevent catastrophe

Introduction

Solar flares are vast eruptions of plasma from the Sun's surface that occur as a result of the Sun's magnetic field lines becoming twisted by the Sun's rotation. Solar flares typically occur between two sunspots, magnetic "storms" on the surface of the Sun. Vector magnetic field measurements of solar flares provide information about the strength and direction of the magnetic fields which generate the flares, and can be used to predict flares and warn airlines flying over polar routes, satellite operators, and communications and broadcasting companies to prepare for the arrival of ions and ionizing radiation.

Predicting solar flares

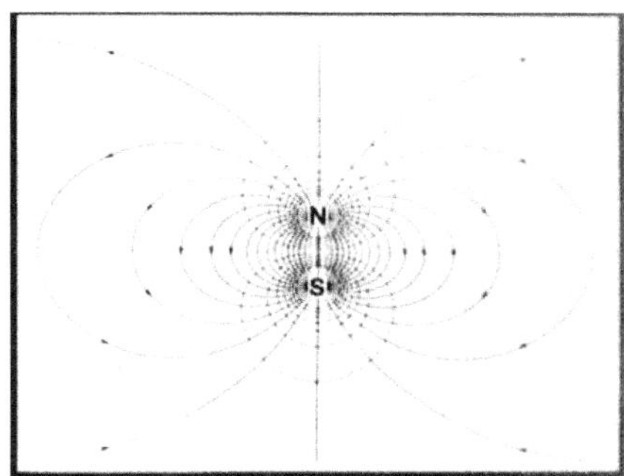

Magnetic lines of force rise from the north pole of a magnet and sink into the south pole of a magnet.

Solar flares are intimately associated with sun spots. Sun spots are disturbances in the Sun's magnetic field that break through to the surface. Magnetic field lines generally stretch from one sun spot to another. But because of the Sun's rotation and the difference in the speed of rotation for different layers and regions of the Sun, the magnetic force lines can become twisted and ultimately shear.

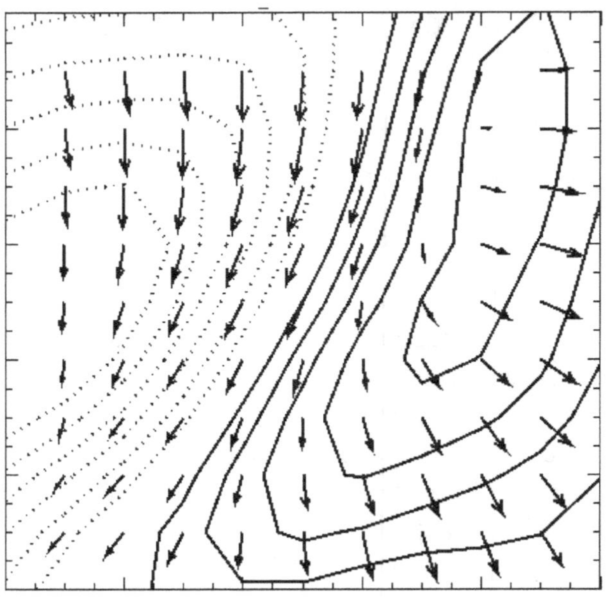

Magnetic field lines on the Sun. Notice the field lines on the right side of the image pointing toward the right, away from the north/south flow. This magnetic field is undergoing shear.

The magnetic field lines can be visualized using vector magnetic field measurements. Light emitted from the Sun at a wavelength of 5250.2 Angstroms (A) is split in two as it passes through the magnetic field of the Sun. The direction of polarization is dependent upon the direction and strength of the magnetic field through which the light passes. Changes in the direction of the magnetic field between sun spots can be visualized. When the magnetic field lines do not point in the direction of the rising or sinking lines emanating from the sun spots, the magnetic field is being twisted. Scientists can measure the degree of shear and predict whether the field will become severed and form a solar flare. However, solar flare prediction is still not reliable. Much more needs to be learned about the mechanisms that cause solar flares.

Preventing catastrophe

When a solar flare occurs, scientists have only a few minutes to hours to warn of its impending arrival. Solar flares damage satellite solar panels, reducing their ability to generate power. Solar panels are designed to be 25% larger at launch than actually needed to account for degradation over time by the Sun's radiation. The impact of a solar flare's particles pushes satellites closer to the Earth. By moving them closer to the Earth, the solar flare reduces the lifespan of the satellite and may cause it to reenter the atmosphere. Satellites must be repositioned after solar flares to account for the loss in orbital altitude. Ions and protons can impact a satellite and create a cascade of electrically charged particles to be released from the walls and other components of the satellite. When enough particles are generated at one time, a "miniature lightning bolt" can form inside the satellite and fry its delicate instrument components.

When a solar flare ejects ions and charged particles into space, they race toward the Earth. The Earth has a strong magnetic field because of its iron core. The particles are deflected from the surface of the planet and race along the magnetic field lines of the Earth to the

Earth's poles. The charged particles racing along the magnetic field lines cause the Earth's magnetic field to vibrate. Magnetic field vibrations generate electrical currents, and can cause power surges along electric power transmission lines of the power grid. Power surges from the ground can also be induced inside transformers. Temperatures inside a transformer can rocket up to 750°F and insulation melts off the lines. Transformers can fail, burst into flame, or explode. These kinds of events cost the power companies billions of dollars every year.

Aircraft fly over the poles on transoceanic flights to shorten the distance they must travel. A flight across the Pacific at the equator would be over 12,000 miles at its widest point. By flying over the poles, airlines take advantage of the fact that the circumference of a sphere decreases as you move toward the poles. Solar flares send charged particles racing along the Earth's magnetic field toward the poles, potentially exposing passengers and crew to dangerous levels of radiation. Aircraft companies divert or cancel polar flights when solar flares occur, costing them tens to hundreds of thousands of dollars for each flight in increased fuel cost or lost revenue.

Scientists use their knowledge of solar flares and the particles and light emissions they create to devise protective shielding for satellites and spaceships. Satellites may be shut down during the flare, and orbits will be checked and satellites repositioned as needed. Scientists warn power companies and radio broadcasters of the impending flare so they can take steps to protect their delicate equipment, including shutting down briefly. Airlines are warned and most decide to cancel or redirect polar flights. There is little else that scientists can do. Solar events are so powerful that it is unlikely that humans will ever develop the technology to control them.

Summary

Solar flares typically occur between two sunspots, magnetic "storms" on the surface of the Sun. Vector magnetic field measurements of solar flares provide information about the strength and direction of the magnetic fields which generate the flares, and can be used to predict flares. Scientists use their knowledge of solar flares to devise protective shielding for satellites and spaceships, and warn power companies, radio broadcasters and airlines of the impending flare so they can take steps to protect their delicate equipment, passengers, and crews.

Concept Reinforcement:

1. How do scientists "see" magnetic field lines on the Sun and measure their direction and strength?

2. How do solar flares damage satellites?

3. How do scientists reduce the damage solar flares do?

Chapter 43 – Understanding Asteroids/Comets

Chapter Objective:

- Explain how scientists measure, monitor and evaluate potential asteroid and comet impacts

Introduction

Impacts from space have recently become a cause of great concern to emergency planners, astrophysicists, and astronomers, as well as the general public. With the announcement by paleontologists that a large object from space crashed into the Earth at about the same time the dinosaurs became extinct, there was a great deal of conjecture that the same thing could happen again. Scientists have located several very large impact craters on the Earth's surface. Recently the hypothesis that the moon was formed after an extremely massive object collided with the Earth has received additional scientific support from observations of lunar rocks.

Although the probability of a collision with a large object is vanishingly small, the potential for a catastrophic collision certainly exists. The magnitude of the disaster that can occur in the event of a collision makes a monitoring program worthwhile. Scientists must measure, monitor and evaluate the potential chance of asteroid and comet impacts so governments can take steps to prevent the extinction of the human species.

Measuring the probability of an impact

The Barringer Impact Crater in Arizona is nearly one mile wide and 570 feet deep.

Scientists look for evidence of impact craters on the surface of the Earth using satellite imagery and aerial photography. They attempt to determine the age of the crater using radiologic dating methods that track the decay of radioactive elements into their decay products. Radioactive decay occurs at a known rate, the half-life of a radioactive isotope. By determining the ratio of the radioactive element to its decay products in a specimen, scientists can estimate the amount of time that has passed.

Scientists also estimate the length of time a crater should remain visible on the planet's surface. The Earth's surface is made up of tectonic plates that move. Some of those plates are pushed below others toward the Earth's mantle where the rocks melt and are eventually recycled to the planet's surface. However, any trace of an impact would be wiped out. If not for tectonic plate actions, the surface of the Earth would look like the surface of the moon.

There are currently 170 known impact craters visible on the planet's surface. Using this information and radioactive dating, scientists estimate that Earth impacts of objects one kilometer (km; 0.6 miles) across or larger occur with a frequency of once every 500,000 years. Objects over 5 km across impact the Earth about once every ten million years. The last object to exceed 10 km impacted the Earth about 65 million years ago.

Monitoring the probability of an impact

The National Aeronautics and Space Administration (NASA) operates the Near Earth Object (NEO) program to monitor and track asteroids and other objects in orbits that allow them to pass close to the Earth. There are 971 known Potentially Hazardous Asteroids, asteroids of sufficient size in orbits sufficiently close to Earth's that a catastrophic collision might occur. NEO Program astronomers capture images of the sky a few minutes apart using CCD cameras similar to the home digital camera, but much more sensitive. These images are compared to one another and moving objects are identified. Once identified, their orbits are calculated and their mass and size are estimated. If they fit the definition of a NEO, NASA tracks them.

Evaluating impacts

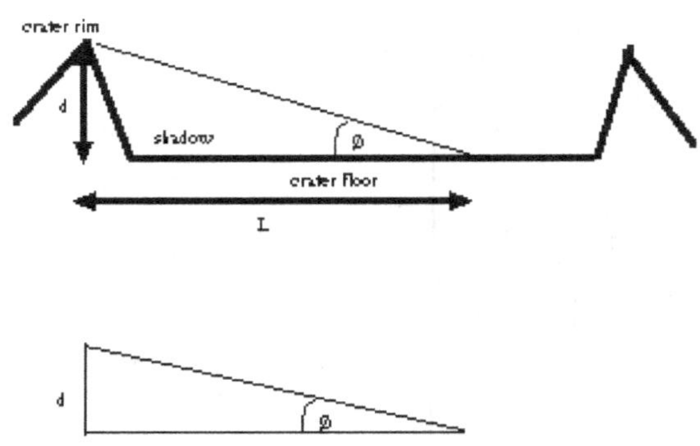

How a crater forms indicates the size, velocity, and angle of impact of an object from space.

Once an impact location is found, scientists drill into the crater to collect core samples. Core samples provide insights into the changes that occurred when the Earth's surface was struck. Layers of soil and rock are blasted off the surface of the planet into the air. The kinetic energy of the object is converted into heat and light energy, melting solid rock and creating new minerals due to the high temperature, similar to what happens in volcanoes. The size of the impact crater gives an approximate boundary to the upper and lower limit of the size of the impact object. The size and shape of the crater, as well as the changes that took place beneath the surface provide information of the angle at which the object struck.

The energy released in an impact can be calculated based on the mass of the object, its velocity, and the angle at which it impacts the Earth. A 5 km asteroid striking the Earth is estimated to create an explosion equivalent to 10,000,000 megatons (670,000,000 Hiroshima bombs) and leave a 95 km wide crater. Fortunately, most explosions happen high in the upper atmosphere and the object never reaches the surface. Even when large objects reach the planet's surface, 71% of the Earth is covered with water, and much of the land is uninhabited, so impacts go unreported and unnoticed.

Summary

Earth impacts of objects one kilometer across or larger occur with a frequency of once every 500,000 years. Objects over 5 km across impact the Earth about once every ten million years. The last object to exceed 10 km impacted the Earth about 65 million years ago. The magnitude of devastation such impacts cause warrants the NEO Program whereby NASA monitors large objects that may impact the Earth at some future date. There are 971 known Potentially Hazardous Asteroids. The energy released in an impact can be calculated based on the mass of the object, its velocity, and the angle at which it impacts the Earth. A 5 km asteroid striking the Earth is estimated to create an explosion equivalent to 10,000,000 megatons and leave a 95 km wide crater.

Concept Reinforcement:

1. Why are there only 170 known impact craters on Earth?

2. How does NASA discover NEOs and decide whether to track them?

3. How do scientists calculate the force of an asteroid collision on Earth?

Chapter 44 – Tracking Asteroid/Comet Paths

Chapter Objective:

- Understand the role science plays in potential asteroid and comet impacts

Introduction

The National Aeronautics and Space Administration (NASA) operates the Near Earth Object (NEO) program to monitor and track asteroids and other objects in orbits that allow them to pass close to the Earth. Additional programs that have been launched to detect and track NEOs include the Lincoln Near-Earth Asteroid Research (LINEAR) program at the Massachusetts Institute of Technology (MIT), the Near-Earth Asteroid Tracking (NEAT) program at the Jet Propulsion Laboratory's (JPL) Mt. Palomar Observatory, and the Lowell Observatory Near-Earth Object Search (LONEOS) in Flagstaff, AZ.

Near Earth Objects (NEOs)

NASA defines a Near Earth Object (NEO) as "… asteroids and comets with perihelion distance q less than 1.3 AU. Near-Earth Comets (NECs) are further restricted to include only short-period comets (i.e orbital period P less than 200 years). The vast majority of NEOs are asteroids…" An AU, or astronomical unit, is equal to the distance from the Earth to the Sun, about 93,000,000 miles. Perihelion is the closest point of approach to the Earth by the object. In short, any object that comes as close as 1.3 times the distance from the Earth to the Sun is considered a NEO.

Discovering NEOs

Astronomers capture images of the sky a few minutes apart using CCD cameras similar to the home digital camera, but much more sensitive. Most of the objects in the images will be stars, and they will not move. Other objects will have moved fractionally. The images are compared to one another and moving objects are identified. Once identified, their orbits are calculated and their mass and size are estimated.

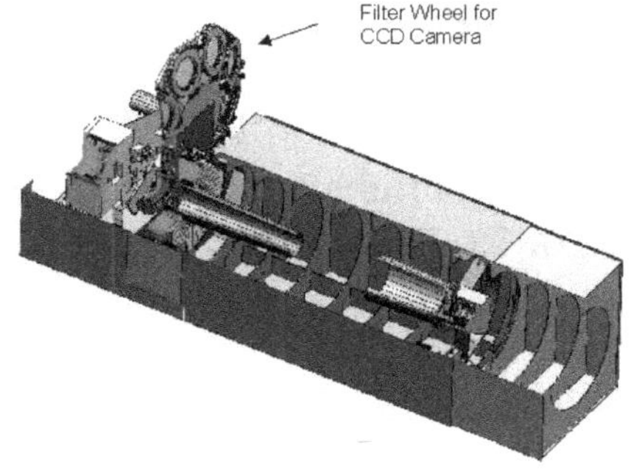

CCD camera

Scientists use the laws of planetary motion and gravity to calculate the paths of NEOs. Astronomers must consider the effects of the Sun's gravity, the gravity of each of the planets, (especially Jupiter), the gravity of the Moon, and the gravity of the three largest asteroids in the Asteroid Belt. This is in addition to the gravity of the Earth itself on a NEO to calculate its most probable orbit. Astronomers and astrophysicists use a complex computer algorithm to calculate the path of the NEO.

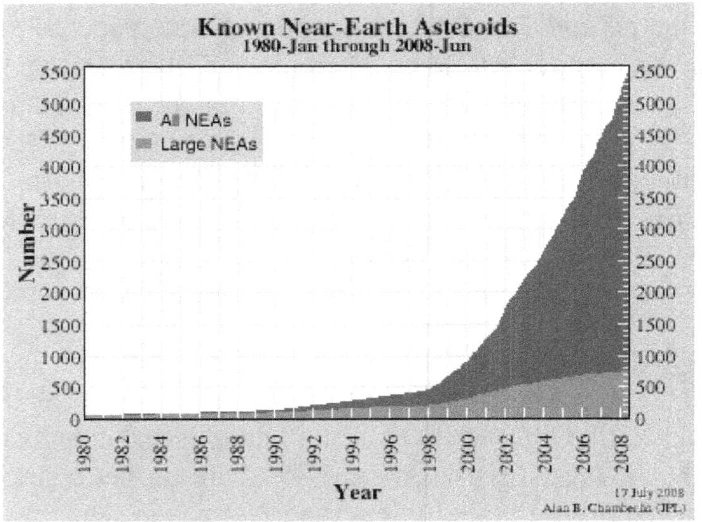

Known Near-Earth Asteroids

If the calculated orbit fits the definition of a Potentially Hazardous Asteroid (PHA), NASA tracks the object. PHAs are asteroids that approach Earth as closely as 0.05 AU (approximately 4,650,000 mi) and are larger than 500 ft in diameter. There are 971 known PHAs, asteroids of sufficient size in orbits sufficiently close to Earth's that a catastrophic collision might occur. Only the objects most likely to impact Earth are tracked daily. Other objects may be tracked once each week or even each month. Objects are tracked as long as they are visible or until they enter the daytime sky.

Developing a response to PHAs

Movies and science fiction books have popularized the notion that an approaching asteroid or other PHA can be blown up, thereby solving the problem of having a large object impact the Earth. Scientists know better. They can directly observe the effects of the impacts of the pieces of comet Shoemaker-Levy 9 on Jupiter in 1994. Twenty-one impacts were observed on Jupiter as a result of that collision. Fireballs reaching temperatures of nearly 43,000°F and plumes reaching to a height of 3,000 km were observed. One collision struck with the force of 6,000,000 megatons of TNT, and two others struck together with a similar force.

Instead of breaking an asteroid into smaller pieces, each of which could have devastating effects, scientists prefer to look for ways to nudge a PHA into a non-threatening orbit. Early detection of a PHA on a collision course with Earth would allow very small forces to be exerted against the asteroid over a long period of time to deflect its orbit sufficiently to miss Earth.

Summary

NASA operates and funds several programs designed to discover and track NEOs. Astronomers calculate their orbits and estimate their sizes using complex mathematical algorithms and high-speed computers. NEOs that will pass within 0.05 AU of the Earth and that are larger than half a kilometer across are tracked by NASA. Scientists are currently experimenting with potential methods of deflecting PHAs so that they will miss the Earth and sail harmlessly off into space.

Concept Reinforcement:

1. How does NASA define a NEO?

2. How does NASA define a PHA?

3. What variables must be considered when calculating the orbit of a NEO?

Chapter 45 – Predicting Asteroid/Comet Impacts

Chapter Objective:

- Analyze how we can use science to predict potential asteroid and comet impacts

Introduction

Scientists use the laws of planetary motion and gravity to calculate the paths of Near Earth Objects (NEOs). Astronomers must consider the effects of the Sun's gravity, the effects of the gravity of each of the planets, especially Jupiter, the effect of the gravity of the Moon, and the gravity of the three largest asteroids in the Asteroid Belt in addition to the gravity of the Earth itself on a NEO to calculate its most probable orbit. Astronomers and astrophysicists use a complex computer algorithm to calculate the path of the NEO.

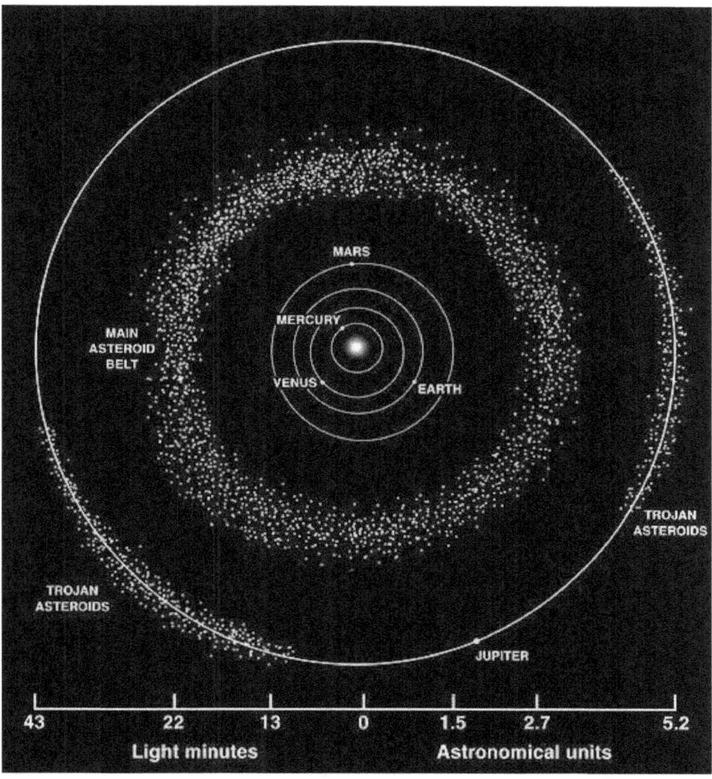

Asteroid Belt

Calculating NEO orbits

Recall that astronomers use CCD cameras to create images of the sky, which are then compared to locate moving objects. If an object is discovered, astronomers and astrophysicists calculate the likely orbit of the object for each image. They then compare the calculated position with the observed position in the next image. The difference between the observed orbit and the calculated orbit is called the residual, (an important mathematical concept beyond the scope of this unit). The calculation for the NEO's orbit is adjusted, and recalculated over several iterations until the sum of squares of the residuals reaches a minimum. This is the "best fit" orbit and is the one used to calculate the potential of the object to intersect the orbit of the Earth. As new observations of the NEO are made, the best fit orbit can be further updated and corrected. Once the orbit has been calculated, a computer algorithm calculates the orbital path of the NEO and the Earth for the next 100 years and hazardously close approaches are listed in the Earth Close Approach tables available on NASA's web site. Approximately 20 close approaches occur each month.

THE TORINO SCALE
Assessing Asteroid/Comet Impact Predictions

No Hazard	**0**	The likelihood of collision is zero, or is so low as to be effectively zero. Also applies to small objects such as meteors and bolides that burn up in the atmosphere as well as infrequent meteorite falls that rarely cause damage.
Normal	**1**	A routine discovery in which a pass near the Earth is predicted that poses no unusual level of danger. Current calculations show the chance of collision is extremely unlikely with no cause for public attention or public concern. New telescopic observations very likely will lead to re-assignment to Level 0.
Meriting Attention by Astronomers	**2**	A discovery, which may become routine with expanded searches, of an object making a somewhat close but not highly unusual pass near the Earth. While meriting attention by astronomers, there is no cause for public attention or public concern as an actual collision is very unlikely. New telescopic observations very likely will lead to re-assignment to Level 0.
	3	A close encounter, meriting attention by astronomers. Current calculations give a 1% or greater chance of collision capable of localized destruction. Most likely, new telescopic observations will lead to re-assignment to Level 0. Attention by the public and by public officials is merited if the encounter is less than a decade away.
	4	A close encounter, meriting attention by astronomers. Current calculations give a 1% or greater chance of collision capable of regional devastation. Most likely, new telescopic observations will lead to re-assignment to Level 0. Attention by the public and by public officials is merited if the encounter is less than a decade away.
Threatening	**5**	A close encounter posing a serious, but still uncertain threat of regional devastation. Critical attention by astronomers is needed to determine conclusively whether or not a collision will occur. If the encounter is less than a decade away, governmental contingency planning may be warranted.
	6	A close encounter by a large object posing a serious, but still uncertain threat of a global catastrophe. Critical attention by astronomers is needed to determine conclusively whether or not a collision will occur. If the encounter is less than three decades away, governmental contingency planning may be warranted.
	7	A very close encounter by a large object, which if occurring this century, poses an unprecedented but still uncertain threat of a global catastrophe. For such a threat in this century, international contingency planning is warranted, especially to determine urgently and conclusively whether or not a collision will occur.
Certain Collisions	**8**	A collision is certain, capable of causing localized destruction for an impact over land or possibly a tsunami if close offshore. Such events occur on average between once per 50 years and once per several 1000 years.
	9	A collision is certain, capable of causing unprecedented regional devastation for a land impact or the threat of a major tsunami for an ocean impact. Such events occur on average between once per 10,000 years and once per 100,000 years.
	10	A collision is certain, capable of causing a global climatic catastrophe that may threaten the future of civilization as we know it, whether impacting land or ocean. Such events occur on average once per 100,000 years, or less often.

Fig. 2. Public description for the Torino Scale, revised from Binzel (2000) to better describe the attention or response that is merited for each category.

Torino Scale

NSA uses two scales to communicate the probability of an impact and the potential de-
duction that will be caused by a collision with an interplanetary object. The Torino scale
designed for public communication. It is color coded and easy to understand. Levels 0
rough 4 warrant no concern by the public. Nearly every NEO assigned to one of these
tegories either poses no risk at all, or is likely to be reassigned to the zero-risk category
additional observations are made. Level 5 through 7 require contingency planning by
tional or international governmental organizations. The risk of an impact large enough
cause significant damage over a fairly large area over a 10 to 100-year period is high.
vels 8 through 10 indicate an impact is certain to occur causing local, regional, or global
aster.

e Palermo scale, on the other hand, is designed for use by NEO specialists. The Palermo
le is a logarithmic scale, so each unit represents a ten-fold increase in risk, not a single
it increase. The Palermo scale compares the likelihood a PHA will impact the Earth with
e likelihood any object of similar size will impact the Earth. If there is no difference be-
een the two probabilities, then the probability of the PHA striking the Earth in a given
ar is no greater than a random chance. The scale ranges from -2 to +2. A -2 rating means
e object is only 1% more likely to strike the Earth than a random object. A +2 rating
ans the object is 100 times more likely than a random object to strike the Earth.

ummary

ientists use the laws of planetary motion and gravity to calculate the paths of NEOs.
tronomers and astrophysicists calculate the likely orbit of the object, and then compare
e calculated position with the observed position in the next image. The resulting "best fit"
bit is used to calculate the potential of the object to intersect the orbit of the Earth. A com-
ter algorithm calculates the orbital path of the NEO and the Earth for the next 100 years
d hazardously close approaches are identified. NASA uses two scales to communicate
e probability of an impact and the potential destruction that will be caused by a collision
th an interplanetary object. The Torino scale is designed for public communication. It is
lor coded and easy to understand. The Palermo scale, on the other hand, is designed for
e by NEO specialists.

---

oncept Reinforcement:

1. How is a best fit orbit calculated?

2. What is the Torino scale and why is it used?

3. What is the Palermo scale and for whom is it intended?